HUNGER

A MEMOIR

BY

MARIAN DEL VECCHIO

LEAPYEAR
PRESS

For Frank, Richard and Angela

Contents

My wickedness I do repent
I really am to blame
And yet if e'er I got the chance
I'd do it all again.

PREFACE

Even though I've recovered from the bulimia that dominated many years of my life, I don't understand it any more than those who attempted to treat it. The eating disorders that were hidden in my day have become commonplace, yet are still as hard to overcome as ever.

In the 1950s, when the prevailing wisdom regarding mental aberrations was Freudian, there was even less understanding but more certitude. Whether one was a kleptomaniac, suicidal, a compulsive hand washer or a secret vomiter didn't really make a difference: the finger of suspicion pointed to one's parents, and of course, one's sexual repressions. Insurance at the time did not cover treatment; those who couldn't afford analysis or one of the nicer mental hospitals either coped as best they could or landed in a state institution. Ironically, those who had to cope on their own were probably no worse off than those of us who were stuck in the Freudian labyrinth.

We were members of "the silent generation." Although there may have been almost as many eating disorders then as there are today, they were in the closet, as I was. For females of my set this was the time of white gloves and low expectations. In college we were expected to look and dress in a way that befitted an ivy leaguer, slim and sleek in the uniform of the time: Bermuda shorts, cardigans, trench coats. This was prior to the pill and the legalization of abortion, dictating a code of virginity before marriage. And marriage was our destiny; we pursued husbands rather than careers.

Fitting in was particularly important in my family. My parents had been uprooted by World War II from their very comfortable European existence, and we children recognized that our job was somehow to help them regain a lost sense of security. Conformity was key; it was doubly important to do the right thing and to look good in the process. My mother's explanation for refusing a requested activity: "It simply isn't done." A woman's role was to be decorative and frivolous.

"Why are you studying," she would say, "A woman's job is to be happy."

But none of this explains my food addiction, and answers to the usual questions lead nowhere.

My parents' insecurities? As a young child I had to look elsewhere for re-assurance, but not for love. I was a happy, skinny child; the eating problem surfaced in my teenage years, unrelated to parental anxieties. *Genetics?* My identical twin sister is no more anorexic than the average New Yorker. *How about the culture of thinness?* As teenagers we aimed to look like magazine models, but there was less emphasis then on food and dieting than there is now. We drank whole milk, used butter, and didn't fret over pesticides. Nobody ever heard of anorexia or bulimia. I was very much alone.

"My God," a friend said recently, after our discussion of eating disorders, "you're a walking compendium of everything psychiatrists did wrong in the fifties – you should write it down." The following story is the result.

Re-reading it at this stage of my life, I wince at those lost years, where I assumed a party girl role, floating in and out of relationships and hospitals with a fake air of insouciance. I'm saddened by the fruitless attempts at treatment, all the good intentions, and all the waste. Though some names are changed, the memories are true, aided by contemporaneous diaries and actual medical records.

As far as my own recovery is concerned, it would never have occurred without the realization that treatment was a dead end and I was on my own. My husband led the way, and I followed.

War

I have the weird distinction of having been an anorexic/bulimic well before the terms entered common usage, enduring and surviving the wide range of treatments available from the '50s through the mid '60s, and emerging, decades later, in one piece and in great health. How did it all start, and why did it all end happily?

Bad timing may have something to do with it. War dominates my early memories like a more powerful parent, one we were all afraid of.

I was born in 1935 in Jihlava, Czechoslovakia. My parents were from similar backgrounds. They came from German-speaking Austrian Jewish families that prospered in a part of the world where Jews were not made to feel inferior. Both of my great-grandfathers owned textile mills. My parents were raised in a world of financial and social security, in homes that included cooks, chauffeurs and chamber music concerts. Neither family was religious. My father's parents were divorced, an unusual occurrence in those days, and one that probably accounted for his anxieties, which dominated our family life, and possibly saved us. In 1938, when Hitler changed everything, my father recognized the danger and managed to get us out. My mother was twenty-seven, my father thirty-eight. They left everything behind. There was money in Switzerland, but nothing else.

More about my family: it includes my older-by-three years brother, Frank, and, of course, my identical twin sister Susan. We were blond, blue eyed, cute, and above all we were "twins," a sensation wherever we went. Poor Frank.

All three of us sensed we were obliged to be happy; it was the least we could do for our parents.

My early history is a mixture of facts and memories.

April, 1938 — We leave for Laurana, Italy, with our nanny, Tetta, and our grandparents, Omi and Opi. My grandfather buys a house by the sea. My father leaves for England to try to arrange an entry permit. Italy becomes fascistic and my family becomes nervous. We move to Switzerland.

Our days are spent running down a long expanse of grass and splashing on a flat gray stone at the dock's edge. The grown-ups have a game: guess which one is Marian, and which one is Susan. I show the brown spot on my hand to prove who I am and make everyone laugh. I feel sorry for Frankie, who is only himself.

Summer, 1938 — We live in a *pensione* in Lausanne, Switzerland. Tetta is let go. My mother is advised we can stay in the country for one year after filing an application. The questions on the application include religion. My father is still in London, having problems with the permit. There is no response to the Swiss application.

Something is wrong, and where is Papa?

December, 1938 — My father has solved the legalities, and we fly to London, where he meets us at the airport. We live in the Dominions Hotel, close to Hyde Park. My mother hires a bilingual governess but instructs her that we are to speak only English.

Our governess wears a hat and has a mean face. She understands German but gets angry when we speak it. My mother explains that if the English hear us speaking German they will think that we are bad, just like the Germans. Frankie gets into trouble for forgetting.

The first governess doesn't work out, and is replaced with a second, Miss Hargreaves.

Everything changes when Hargreaves arrives. Hargreaves is tall and has light colored hair. She teaches us to sit straight at the table, eat with a fork, not make "personal remarks" and curtsey because we might meet the Queen. She takes us for walks in Hyde Park, where we watch boys sail their boats in the pond. Each night Hargreaves brushes our hair, counting each stroke, and tells us stories.

March, 1939 — Invasion of Czechoslovakia and outbreak of war in England. Children are evacuated from London to the suburbs. We move to a boarding house in Southport, Hargreaves' hometown. Southport is a lovely suburb on the coast, and my grandfather buys a house by the sea.

Opi's house has big windows that open out to a garden. We sit in the garden with Hargreaves, who teaches us to draw letters. Inside the house, she plays the piano, while we become ballerinas and dance.

Somewhere along the line we three children are baptized in the Anglican Church.

1940 — France falls, and the war looks lost. Hitler is now in Czechoslovakia, Austria, Denmark, Norway, Luxembourg, the Netherlands, Belgium and France. An invasion is expected in England, very likely at Southport. Ours is the house closest to the beach, and my mother expects to wake up to the sound of storm troopers. A doctor provides her with enough cyanide pills for the family. At this point a permit to the US is impossible. My father leaves for Liverpool to work on passage to South America.

There is a hut in the garden. Susan and I pretend it is ours. At night the same bad dream begins. I dream that Papa is trying to find us but can't because we are laughing and playing too far away to hear him calling our names. When I wake up I feel very sad.

My father lives in a Liverpool hotel while trying to arrange our passage. He eats in its dining room at night, where he listens to some old English dowagers talk. He remembers their exact words: "What these people don't understand is the might of the British Navy!" The only man in the group, whom my father recognizes as a fellow refugee, outdoes their fervent assurances that the British Navy will prevail. The man and my father never talk. One evening, after the ladies depart, the man looks around to make sure they are gone. Turning slightly in my father's direction he remarks, "Look into the sun. Don't think, or you'll go crazy."

Where is Papa? I feel very sad.

Getting a special Capitalist Visa to Brazil requires a certain amount of money, a seemingly insurmountable hurdle, as it is illegal to take money out of England during wartime. My father moves to London to try to resolve this, and we join him there.

We live in a boarding house owned by the mother of Lilli Palmer, the actress and movie star. Rex Harrison is a frequent visitor.

The old lady who owns the house understands German. Her daughter ignores us, even though we are cute and no one can tell us apart.

When the blitz starts, the Brits carry on without panic. Everyone goes about business as usual. We sleep in a basement shelter at night. My father sees planes shot down, but doesn't know if they are German or English. In the morning my brother goes into the garden to collect the shells.

Frankie gets to go to the garden and bring back stuff I don't understand.

"The British are wonderful," my father repeats several times. They have allowed him to take out the required funds for the Visa.

Travel to Brazil is arranged with great secrecy. We are simply told to move to Liverpool and await instructions. The only available rooms in the Liverpool hotel are on the top floor, fifteen flights up, the worst in the event of an air raid. There is a terrible raid our first night there. My father carries one twin, my mother another, and my brother walks. We spend the night in a Turkish bath transformed into a shelter.

Mommy is wearing her pretty yellow dress that ties behind, but something is wrong. Somebody is carrying me, and I wake up in a place that has curtains. Where is Mommy? She appears, wearing her yellow dress, but her face is sad.

The next day we are told to go to a certain pier and "await instructions."

September, 1940 — We board the Almeda Star, a splendid liner normally used for passenger and cargo service between the UK and South America. Although designed for 200 passengers, there are only eighteen aboard on its current mission, which is to bring back military supplies from Argentina. We expect to depart that night, but there is a terrible attack, with bombs barely missing the ship. The next morning we awake to find we are out at sea, part of a convoy of ships. For two days we are part of the convoy; the third we are alone. We're on a zigzag course designed to throw off the enemy, up to the Arctic, then South. It will take three weeks to get to Rio.

My mother later recalls, with amusement, that once aboard, Susan's first question was "where is the playground?" and mine was "where are the lifeboats?" Among the other passengers are two young English girls. Traveling alone, they are being sent to relatives in South America.

The two girls, our new friends, are lucky because they get to choose their own clothes. Captain Howard is a magic man. He can pull eggs out of hats and my hankie out of his elbow. It is very funny and makes us all laugh.

Although my father has warned my mother not to give us baths, she decides to do so, one at a time. During my bath a steward looks in, his face white. "We're going into battle." My mother grabs me and we join the others on deck, next to the lifeboats. To everyone's relief the unidentified plane disappears.

First the grown-ups are scared, and then they are happy.

October, 1940 — We arrive in Rio. Our picture is in the October 7 edition of *O Globo*, with a feature article describing the dangerous journey. The photo shows my sister and me holding little suitcases and stuffed animals, with Frank standing behind us.

ANNO XVI — N. 4427   Segunda-feira, 7 de outubro de 1940

O GLOBO

FUNDAÇÃO DE IRINEU MARINHO

Director-Thesoureiro   Director-Redactor-Chefe   Director-Gerente
HERBERT MOSES   ROBERTO MARINHO   A. LEAL DA COSTA

"DERROTAREMOS HITLER ONDE ELLE ESTIVER!..., — O "Almeda Star" e o "Lalande", o grande trans-
t!antico da Blue Star Line, e o cargueiro de Lamport, vieram de Liverpool, sem qualquer novidade. O commandant
do "Lalande", capitão William Gough, que se vê na gravura, falando ao reporter, accentuou sua fé inabalavel no
destinos das armas inglezas. Tambem na gravura apparecem Suzanne e Marianne, duas encontadoras filhinhas do in
dustrial tcheco Gan Seidner, e de sua esposa, Sra. Alice Seidner, passageiros do "Almeda Star". Frans Seidner, ir-
mão de Suzanne e Marianne, tambem apparece na "cliché" (Ler mais na 2.ª pagina).

"WE SHALL DEFEAT HITLER — EVERYWHERE!" — The Almeda
Star, the big transatlantic steamer of the Blue Star Line, and the Lalande, a
Lamport cargo ship, have arrived from Liverpool, with no incidents to report.
The Lalande's Captain, William Gough, seen in this photogravure speaking to
reporters, emphasized his faith in the British Armed Forces. In the same illustra-
tion we see Suzanne and Marianne, charming young daughters of Czech industrialist Jan Seidner and his wife Madame Alice Seidner, passengers aboard the
Almeda Star. Frans Seidner, the brother of Suzanne and Marianne, can be seen
in the picture.

7 October, 1940

O GLOBO

"WE SHALL DEFEAT HITLER — EVERYWHERE!"

Just arrived today from the British Isles, are the Almeda's young passengers, after crossing from London to Rio.

The cargo ship Lalande of the Lamporte Holt Company, which reportedly had been torpedoed and sunk, arrived this morning at Guanabara from Liverpool with stops in Cardiff and the State of Bahia. The British Merchant Marine vessel is well known in Rio — and the ship's route, established for several years, was a routine crossing with nothing of note to be reported.

"It was as if it were peace time" said Captain William Gough speaking from the bridge.

Captain William Gough, well known to the press corps, greeted journalists with a gracious smile. In no way did he evade their questions. We reminded him of his earlier statements when the ship had stopped at Salvador de Bahia. Captain Gough shows total confidence in the victory of British forces.

"Hitler up to now did as he liked in Europe. However the turning point has arrived. Now with Britain in the war, everything has changed."

He concludes with a smile. "We have now got Hitler where we want him."

We were descending the stairs when the Captain added: "I almost forgot to mention...English bombing raids have done more damage to Germany than German raids on England."

And he repeated: "We English will take Hitler where we want him, and we will defeat him everywhere."

In addition to 2000 tonnes of cargo, the Lalande carried to Rio two purebred stallions belonging to a Carioca horse breeder.

"Children arrived from London"

In spite of everything, the Almeda Star made an uneventful crossing from Liverpool to Rio, after over 18 days at sea. The Blue Star Line transatlantic steamer, powerfully armed with three rapid fire cannon as well as anti-aircraft guns, transported 13 passengers to the capital. Of note among them was Czech industrialist Jan Seidner, who made the crossing with his wife Alice Seidner and their three young children, Franz, eight years old, and Suzanne and Marianne, five year old twins.

These happy, smiling little children, the youngest passengers on board, had fortunately overcome all the perils in the journey from their homeland to England. Now, they arrive in Rio from London, accompanied by their parents, carrying the toys they brought from Europe.

January 17, 1941 — On her next trip the Almeda Star is torpedoed by a German U-Boat. She sinks without a trace.

※ ※ ※

Rio — The days are white with heat. We live in a modern apartment building on Copacabana Beach, with a live-in maid and a nanny. We go to a British private school on the Rua Santa Clara in Copacabana. My father walks us to school in the morning.

I love Rio, where the pavements have pretty patterns and the grown-ups are happy. Auchina, our maid, sings and swings her hips. Our nanny, Gloria, speaks English and tells us true stories about circus acrobats who fall off tight ropes and are eaten by tigers. In the afternoon she takes us to the playground, where the children play games. A little girl asks us, in a language we don't understand, to join in the games. Our nanny answers and the girl comes back with more girls. They point fingers at us and call us "Inglese."

Every morning Papa takes us to school, where everyone speaks English. We learn to draw a flag with a circle and stars in it, and we fill white sheets of paper with different letters. Drawing is easy, and we get gold stars on our papers to show they are good.

We go to the beach, where the happy grown-ups play games. We watch them throw a big ball across a net, laughing.

Mommy and Papa are sitting with a man. Mommy tells us he is Brazilian, which means he was born in Brazil. This can't be true. He is a grown-up—how could he still be living in the same place?

❄ ❄ ❄

GOOD NEWS! WE ARE going to a country where everyone speaks English.

July 1941 — We arrive in the USA.

New York City — Our parents send us to a public school, where the teacher tells them we would adjust better if we dropped our English accents. We learn to say "braid" for "plait," "elevator" for "lift," and "you're welcome," for "think nothing of it."

We are the only children in first grade who can't tell the teacher where we live. She takes us to the window and asks us to point. We don't know where to point.

The children in our new country are rude. They are loud and talk back to their parents.

We are in the street and hear an air raid siren. Mommy says we don't have to run to a shelter because the noise is from a big car called an ambulance. There is no war here.

DECEMBER 7, 1941 — Pearl Harbor
Pearl Harbor is a woman we are all supposed to remember.

HUNGER

When did it start? When describing my childhood the first person singular never comes into play—it's always "we" or "our"—in fact it wasn't my childhood, it was ours. Did we compete? With others, absolutely: we had to prove we were smarter, could draw better and run faster than the others. Did we compete with each other? Absolutely not: we were a team, and as a team we were unbeatable in every department, and we took the resulting adulation and applause for granted. We were repeatedly voted "most popular," and we exerted power in our choice of friends and enemies. Separately, it might have been different, but we were inseparable.

"Hey, Twin, which one are you, Susan or Marian?" It didn't matter.

Poor Frankie was separate. He was three years older and knew more than we did: "If you think the first grade is hard, wait until you get to the fourth." Poor Frankie. The teacher said he had bad penmanship. He wanted a sled but didn't ask for one. They were always telling him to stand straight, to take his hands out of his pockets, to speak clearly, to comb his hair. He never answered back. He wasn't a twin, he wasn't cute, nobody seemed especially proud of him.

Not like us. We were perfect, we were twins, we woke up happy and went to bed happy.

"Poor Mommy," Daddy said, every time Mommy vacuumed. "Your poor mother," when she came back from the store with groceries. It was sad that she had to take care of us, cook, and iron our clothes. It was sad that we had to live in an apartment where we could hear our next-door neighbors. Mommy and Daddy knew they had accents and didn't fit in. We did too, and hoped they wouldn't show up at school for Parents' Day.

Daddy was often angry, but he was funny. At the dinner table we roared with laughter when he imitated our friends.

"I'm Janie," he minced in a high-pitched voice, contorting his face and holding his head in a weird way, "I'm little Janie, and my head hurts, and I want my Mommy." Uproarious laughter. "Now I'm Doris," squinting his eyes, and hunching his shoulders, "and I know where your mother bought those napkins."

We laughed until we cried.

"Alice," turning to our mother, "this cake is good, but not as good as Katie Ney's," winking at us. Alice was not amused, which made us all laugh harder.

At home there were differences nobody else knew about. I was the bad one. I was bad but I was funny, so I was like Daddy. I could yell and talk back and make Daddy smile and wink because I was just like him. Susan was the good one, just like Mommy. She was a little angel who never had temper tantrums. I knew that Mommy liked her better, because when Susan said a bad thing and Mommy said "take that back" Susan took it back. I never took it back.

In the playground our friend Sandra Witty asked us, "Are you Catholic, Protestant or Jewish?"

"What?"

Sandra asked the same question again so we could remember it. We returned home.

"Are we Catholic, Protestant or Jewish?" They looked at each other.

"You're Protestant."

What was being Protestant, and what was the secret?

"Are you Protestant too?"

"No"

"What are you?"

"We're Jewish, but it doesn't matter."

We told Sandra we were "Protestant" but we didn't tell her Mommy and Daddy were something else.

They started sending us to the Holy Rood Church every Sunday. It was a twenty-minute walk down Fort Washington Avenue, but we could walk there ourselves, with Frankie. We had to wear hats, so Mommy bought us plaid skirts with matching hats.

At church we kneeled on stools. Frankie was an acolyte, and when we saw him walking down the aisle in a white and black costume it was hard not to giggle.

The priest said things and everyone said things back. After a while we learned the words.

Sunday School was boring and nobody listened to the lesson.

When Mommy said good night I confessed I didn't believe in God. She told me the important thing was to believe in goodness.

One summer we vacationed at Lake Minnewaska, where we stayed at a Quaker resort hotel. Susan and I sat on a porch swing, giggling.

"Be quiet," Daddy said, "it's Sunday, and they'll say 'those foreigners are making a racket.'"

The reason we decided we were adopted was that we had blue eyes and they didn't.

❀ ❀ ❀

PS 187 WAS ACROSS the street, close enough to see from our sixth floor window. Being new girls in the first grade, class One-A, was not a problem.

We're twins, we're smart, we know how to read, to draw, to skip rope, to run fast and remember what the teacher says. School is easy and full of friends. We don't need friends, we have each other.

At school the song we stood up to sing was not about God Save the King but about bombs bursting in air.

We collected paper and tin cans and finished what was on our plate. Mommy mixed yellow into something to make it look like butter and Doris Nathan saved her bubble gum at the end of the day by wrapping it in wax paper.

"Over there, over there, the Yanks are coming, the Yanks are coming, and we won't be back 'til it's over, over there..."

War isn't here, it's there, over there, and it won't come back 'til it's over, over there.

During air raid drills we sat at our window and watched the searchlights practice searching the sky.

✳ ✳ ✳

MRS. SHAPIRO, MISS BUTLER, Mrs. Costello. Mrs. Flanagan.

Mrs. Costello, our teacher in fourth grade, doesn't know they don't speak Spanish in Brazil. Should I raise my hand? Teachers don't know everything.

School is fun, but we all have to wait while the teacher explains things to dopey kids like Tommy Cahill.

✳ ✳ ✳

IN THE FOURTH GRADE we formed a club with our friends Gaby, Carol, Doris and Jane. Our after school activities included jumping rope, bike riding, teasing doormen, and, whenever we spotted one, following a spy.

Maybe the man we're following is not a spy, although he's scary looking and has a German accent. It's hard to keep track of spies, as they usually walk too far for us to follow, but one day we'll stop one from doing something wrong.

✳ ✳ ✳

IN ASSEMBLY WE STOOD at attention and pledged allegiance "to the flag and to the country for which it stands, one nation indivisible, with liberty and justice for all."

Susan and I spent hours cutting confetti out of colored paper to have ready for the end of the war, saving it in paper bags.

August 14, 1945 — VJ Day. We were away when it happened, at a place called Delaware Water Gap. Mommy and Daddy sat there quietly.

Our confetti's at home in the closet, but it doesn't matter. It's too quiet for confetti.

❋ ❋ ❋

IT WAS FUN GOING to see Omi and Opi in the Franconia, their hotel near Central Park. An elevator man took us to the sixteenth floor. The floors skipped thirteen, going eleven, twelve, fourteen, fifteen, sixteen, "because thirteen is bad luck and nobody wants it."

Omi was always busy, sewing at her machine, knitting, or crocheting. She taught us the easy way to make dolls. Opi took his oil set and painted pictures in the park while Omi watched us play.

Back in the hotel Omi scolded Opi for the oil stains on his clothes, while he winked at us and sang songs, "Oh, she was sitting on my knee, while the boys were having tea, and it was B-E-A-U-T-I-F-U-L, and it was beautiful…"

Their hotel room was full of paintings, some by Opi, some by Corot and Courbet. When Opi woke up from his afternoon nap, he told us stories about Van Gogh, Rembrandt and Gauguin.

Opi made us laugh.

At home there was always talk about food.

"Katie's coffee is too weak but her linzer torte was delicious." "How's the sauce? Too much salt?"

Couldn't they think about something else?

"Gideon's Bakery uses too much vanilla. The cakes are awful, though the rolls are okay."

They made me so angry.

"Finish your plate or no dessert."

I tried not to listen.

Why did I get so angry when Susan didn't?

Even though no one could tell us apart I knew Susan was prettier.

When I was eleven my mother took me to the doctor because I couldn't sleep at night.

The Barnard School for Girls

Seventh grade at PS 187. The girls in our class started wearing lipstick and hanging out at the corner drugstore. We envied our friend Gabi, whose parents had switched her from PS 187 to a private school, the Barnard School for Girls. At Barnard the girls weren't allowed to wear makeup or streak their hair, and they wore uniforms. They studied harder and learned more.

We entered the eighth grade at Barnard in 1948, joining a class of nineteen girls in blue serge jumpers and white blouses, who curtsied to the teacher at the end of the day. This was a far cry from PS 187—everyone worked hard, listened in class, showed respect for the teachers—and there were no boys passing notes and whispering in the back of the room. Our eighth grade teacher never raised her voice. Susan and I had to catch up in our study of Latin and French, but that was no problem, and we soon established ourselves as leaders.

We all complain about our uniforms, but I really like mine. I'm glad, walking home by the corner drugstore, that I look different from the girls that hang out there. We say hello and talk, but we're not friends anymore. Mommy calls them cheap, which makes me mad.

Barnard High, which we entered the following fall, was one flight up in the same brick building. Every Wednesday morning before classes began we all sat in the main assembly hall, where Mrs. Gillette, the principal, surveyed the room. Even the teachers were scared of Mrs. Gillette. She had gray hair, a big bosom, skinny legs, and she stared at us through round glasses attached to a black rope.

"You," Mrs. Gillette said in her scary Southern accent, pointing to the new girl in the second row. "You. Stand up. What did you do to your hair?"

The girl stood up. She had a blond streak.

"We don't do that at Barnard."

Mrs. Gillette's pronouncements, always issued in the same steely manner, were never challenged. We were not to wear navy blue or black, unsuitable for young ladies of our age group. Adlai Stevenson was a divorced man, unsuitable for the Presidency.

Ha, ha, about the navy blue and black. What are we supposed to do, wear pink and white? Ha, ha. I don't care what she says; Adlai Stevenson is going to be President.

At the beginning of each assembly the Head of Student Government made a little speech, one of the seniors read from the bible in French, and another senior gave a two-minute talk on any subject, a requirement of senior year. Speech was very important at Barnard, and Miss Sutton, our Speech teacher, taught us to project from the diaphragm. "Hence, home, you idle creatures, get you home," we intoned, or "willows whiten, aspens quiver, little breezes dusk and shiver," without any trace of a New York accent.

We had to stay up late each night doing our homework.

"Why are you working so hard," Mommy said. "The important thing for a woman is to be happy."

I wish she were happy! Anyway, the important thing for a woman to be happy is to look good. She looks pretty good, for her age, considering the amount of cakes and chocolates she eats…though it doesn't matter at her age.

I'd be happy if only I could be really skinny.

Being smart was very important at Barnard, and we had to work hard to maintain our position at the top of the class. Frankie, who was in the Barnard School for Boys, scoffed at our efforts. He managed to get good grades barely cracking a book, but we weren't surprised. Maybe he didn't stand up straight or speak clearly, but they were wrong about Frankie and we knew it. He was the smartest.

With the exception of our glamorous French teacher, Mademoiselle De Nouey, most of our teachers at Barnard were teetering on the brink of senility. Sweet old Mrs. Hoffman, our English teacher, had us read "The Loon Feather" because she "so enjoyed it as a girl." One assignment she gave was to make a color chart of the colors mentioned in "The Ancient Mariner." In spite of her weird teaching practices, we were all fond of Mrs. Hoffman, and behaved well in her classes. One morning she looked out the window and remarked, "I'd love to see all you young girls dancing on a pretty lawn in white dresses, waving green scarves." Nobody laughed.

Mrs. Colby, who taught social studies, scrawled interminable outlines on the blackboard for us to memorize. Her forgetfulness gave us great pleasure; she would often forget assignments and, on occasion, she'd forget her classes altogether.

Sophomore year Mrs. Hoffman retired, and a new young English teacher appeared on the scene. Miss Carroll was in her twenties, very plain, and, it was rumored, a Phi Beta from Smith. It was immediately apparent Miss Carroll loved her subject. She wrote page comments on our papers, and if she liked them, the margins were filled with scrawls of 'EXCELLENT!' She was equally dismayed with how little we knew and how little time she had to teach us; her solution was an impossible amount of homework. For our exam, she expected us to be able to identify every poem in our Untermeyer anthology by title and author. We all cheated on our exam, but we learned our poetry.

Father's Day proved to be poor Miss Carroll's undoing. It was a day when fathers were invited to classes, and her anxiety intensified as the day approached. When the big day arrived, three or four hapless fathers sat in the back of the classroom. Miss Carroll greeted them enthusiastically, then placed a white lamb-shaped cake on her desk.

"This lamb," Miss Carroll explained, "is an offering to the muse. When I call your name please read your poem." After each of us finished reading, we were presented with a slice of the cake. There was then a moment of silence, during which Miss Carroll stared intently into space. Then she began to chant, "What'll we do with the incense pot? Put it in the aisle, it's too damn hot." Though we were a historically troublesome class, nobody laughed, and a few joined in the chanting to make it seem a joke. Someone came and escorted her out of the room. A short time later, Mrs. Hoffman returned to the call of duty, and English classes became, once again, a comfortable bore.

Those four years went by slowly. We worried about our homework, about our skin, about going out on dates, about "how far to go" on a date, and, of course, about our weight. We dated boys from Collegiate, Horace Mann, Riverdale, and, eventually, Columbia University.

We brought classmates home after school, where Mommy was waiting to give us a snack and then leave us alone. They were good about leaving us alone, not like Gabi's parents, who nagged and made her telephone all the time.

I guess we're pretty lucky, as far as parents are concerned. They're not worriers, like a lot of other parents, and, thank God, they don't talk to us about sex.

Mommy often sat on the living room couch, eating Barton's chocolates and playing solitaire. It made my skin crawl.

Why can't she just go on a diet, instead of talking about it. Those chocolates are disgusting. I'm staying away from the refrigerator.

At Barnard we all ate lunch together in the downstairs cafeteria, where we were served the hot lunch of the day. Usually it was pretty good, with rolls and a dessert, like tapioca pudding, chocolate cake, or even ice cream. Carol Bradley, who was on a diet, brought her own lunch in a bag: hard-boiled eggs and cottage cheese.

We noticed that the skinny girls, like Mary Jane O'Connell, put everything on their plates but didn't eat it all. The dieters, like us, tried to take less but wiped our plates clean. Carol Bradley was smart.

Susan was prettier and had more boy friends, or, at least she hung on to them longer. She was dating Jerry Landauer, the editor of Spectator, the Columbia newspaper. When I went out with Art Lebb, Jerry's friend, we had nothing to say to each other.

Most important was looking good. Often I liked what I saw in the mirror; often I didn't. If you really looked good you could attract boys without being interesting. Looking interesting did the trick, and on good days I did.

Being skinny makes my cheekbones show and my eyes look bigger.

Ruth Farley, the prettiest girl in the class, knew the best way to meet boys and have fun: Mrs. Miller's dances, attended by boys and girls from the best prep schools. "Were we Jewish?"

"No." An honest answer but it didn't feel right. What were we?

"Good. Then I'll give her your names."

Daddy hired a car to drive us to the dances. He did it as a convenience, but the uniformed driver impressed the crowd at Mrs. Miller's.

What were we? Fakes.

The Grand Tour

And then the letter came.

We didn't know our mother's older brother until he invited us, sight unseen, on a grand European tour. We were seventeen, and entering our junior year at Barnard. It was 1952, a time when America had saved the world, Truman was in office, and the girls at Barnard were fined a quarter for wearing the wrong color socks with their uniforms.

A photo of Richard Hanak showed squinty eyes behind round glasses, an oversized mouth grinning from protruding ear to protruding ear, a flat nose in a round face, and thinning hair slicked straight back. Undeniably ugly, yet there was something appealingly crazy about that grin, and the letter he wrote my mother was promising. In it he asked, "What do seventeen year old girls do? Can they drink?"

We did our schoolwork, painted our nails, packed our bags, and waited for the big day to arrive. It finally came, and there we were, boarding the *Ile de France*, and, *euphoria*: kissing our parents goodbye.

We watched them go and felt the weight of their world disappear into the blue. We were alone, nobody knew who we were, and we were off to meet the unknown Richard and his equally unknown wife, Wynne. We bought cigarette holders, lied through our teeth, had a great time on board, and arrived in Southampton thoroughly sophisticated and ready for action.

A tall elegantly dressed young woman approached us at the station in London.

"I expect you're Susan and Marian," she said. "I'm Wynne." Wynne told us to call our grandparents, who were in Huddersfield with Richard, and tell them we were going to the opera. "We are actually," she said, "going to dinner and dancing with my young friend Jimmy Batt. Jimmy is a British guard, terribly handsome, and one of you is guaranteed to fall in love. He is, I can assure you, a great catch." Jimmy joined us for drinks at the Mayfair Hotel. He was surely a catch, but it seemed he had already been caught: Wynne and he appeared to have shared more than a few drinks together.

Where was Richard, and what was going on here? But who really cared? We were having Pimms Number One at a London hotel, we were going on to dinner and dancing, our Aunt Wynne was young, no prude, and, above all, our Aunt Wynne knew how to have a good time. This was going to be a grand vacation.

Next stop: Huddersfield, Yorkshire, where Richard owned a textile mill and a home, pompously labeled Bankfield. It all proved to be a far cry from New York and the Barnard School for Girls. A pretty young maid served our breakfast by French windows overlooking rock gardens, flowers, and picturesque fields. At night we put our shoes out for Henry, the chauffeur, to shine.

The war was over in the States, but not here. Food shortages, ration stamps, war stories. Wynne muttered she would have to get rid of the pretty young maid, a German, because she carried hot dishes without potholders, "just like a Nazi."

Wynne lectured us about nail polish, perfume, and wiles to use attracting men, with demonstrations whenever a specimen appeared in our midst—and appear they did—wherever she went, in the wake of her Shalimar perfume. If she was a bit too friendly, as with the good looking bobby in town, we pretended not to notice. When Richard left for work, Wynne drove us around town. We were her "twin nieces from the USA, here for the grand tour, and to break hearts all over Europe." We were her props, and we were proud of it.

THE GRAND TOUR:

July 19-21 — Paris. Stayed at the Hotel Scribe. Champs Elysee, Folies Bergeres, St. Germaine de Pres, Montmartre…phenomenal restaurants, jazz in dark cellars, Rumpelmeyers, Café de La Paix, Laurent, Notre Dame…dancing with French strangers in a Left Bank cellar…Wynne at the bar, Richard in the background.

July 22-23 — Zurich. The lake, the Swiss, the calm.

July 24-26 — Interlacken. Stayed at the Victoria-Jungfrau…swimming in a pool surrounded by snow capped mountains…Grindelwald….flying through the sky on the "first-bahn"… hiking through fresh smelling woods…lunch of fresh trout at the "Blausee."

July 27-30 — Zermatt. Stayed at the Zermatterhoff…narrow streets… mountaineers…no tourists, (i.e., no Americans; 'Europeans are not 'tourists,' they are 'on vacation.') The Matterhorn…*Ripplealp…gluwine*…men and music and walks up steep green paths.

July 31 - August 5 — Venice. Stayed at the Excelsior Lido Hotel. Starry nights, black water, white lights…water, water…the Doges Palace, white moonlight…St Mark's Square, St. Mark's Church, the Florian Café… the music and the singing…lunch at the Hotel Gritti overlooking the canal…the gondolas, always the sound of music…the gala dinner at the Excelsior next to the fountain spouting rainbows…the gowns, the beach, the Biennale…floating through the Grand Canal with palaces and music everywhere.

August 5-7 — Misurina in the Dolomites. Our new handsome chauffeur, Verna Ublemann. Walking uphill and picking edelweiss. Wynne late at night searching the street, calling "Verna," not noticing us following behind. Richard's extravagant tips and laughter…the endless partying.

People wondered who and what we were. "She must be an older sister, but who's he, a Swiss guide?" We laughed; Richard was not amused.

August 8-15 — Bolzano…Lago di Carezza…Madonna di Campligio… Pontresina…Zurich.

August 16 — Back to Bankfield. Just in time for *Party Preparations*.

They didn't really need a reason for a party, but here we were, too good a reason to pass up.

The Hanaks invite you

to a party
given for their twin nieces
Susan and Marian Seidner
from New York

to take place at Bankfield, Taylor Hill
on Saturday, September 6th at 8 p.m.

Food, drinks, films, games, surprises

An early reply requested

Richard's Invitation

We were ordered to do a huge mural of ourselves, the twin nieces from New York, to decorate the party room wall. With jazz in the background to set the mood, we went to work, dancing, painting, happy to oblige. The gigantic mural that emerged, of two twins dancing, definitely passed muster. It was one of our finer works.

Richard was actively engaged rehearsing an opera he composed for the occasion. The theme was in our honor. A program was produced.

The "Bankfield" Opera House,
Bankfield, Taylor Hill, Huddersfield

●

The "Bankfield" Opera Trust

present

The Hanak Opera Company

●

Saturday, September 6th, 1952

at approx. 12.0 midnight

COLUMBUS

Opera in one Act
Libretto by Richard Hanak

Christopher Columbus	Bob Askew
Isabela Queen of Spain	Wynne Hanak
Pedro the Sailor Man	Ben Cederbring
The Virgin of the Moon	Anne Briggs
Her Father Big-Chief	George Emmott

Opera Program

FROM "MY TRIP" JOURNAL:

September 9, 1952 —

Of course we were late to our own party—the first guests arrived
ahead of us—what a rush! We both looked amazing—I wore my pink
and Susan wore her striped. Wynne lent me gold shoes.

The party was a whirl. We had our choice of men; English girls are so reserved. I was in love with all of them, but mainly interested in Jimmy Batt. He jokingly asked me to marry him and I accepted. Ben was at the bar and he kept shoving sherry at me…I was falling more and more madly in love with Jimmy and myself—especially Jimmy. We slipped out into the garden—it was wonderful. The stars, the scent of flowers, echoes of laughter and music from the house. When we returned Wynne jokingly asked if I showed Jimmy the waterfall. Embarrassing.

London with Wynne, 1952

The next morning, a big breakfast for everyone who stayed. Then Jimmy and his friend Milford took us to a pub, 'The Golden Cock' for drinks. Lunch at the George, then Chatsworth, with its lovely gardens.

Got home late and tired, no time to pack. In the morning, chaos and Hell! We managed to shove everything into the trunks, but in the car, we looked for our ten pounds, and *bloody hell,* they were missing. So were our passports! Wynne going crazy, but then, eureka, we found our passports!

"I felt terrible about the money, but Wynne was great. She said it didn't help to worry—she'd just have to borrow the money from Sir Anthony Linsey Hock, a bastard. We sort of cheered up. Back to the Mayfair, where we got the royal treatment, because, Wynne said, 'we're steady customers'. In our room she called up Sir Anthony and kept calling him a bastard and *dahling* in one breath. He asked her to dinner, she accepted, then swore at us for making her go to dinner with a bastard. She said it wasn't safe, and she'd have to call a third. She then called Lord Lawrence, or "Nicky," and cooled off when he said he'd make it.

September 10–15 —

The Queen Elizabeth: The most exciting experience ever. From the very beginning to the end. Thane Parker, the British producer, met us at the station to say goodbye. We'd only met him once, with Wynne, so that was a surprise. He told us his friend, Frederick Knott, would look us up on board. Knott is the playwright who wrote Dial M for Murder, a smash in London, on its way to New York with Maurice Evans. Wynne really gets around! Poor Richard.

A fantastic trip. Parties, parties, parties.

When it's over we'll be back in Barnard.

On board the R.M.S. Queen Elizabeth, 1952

How depressing.

And back we were. Back to our nineteen classmates, our homework, our worries about our skin, dates, boys, and weight. The glamour gone as fast as it had come.

Wynne's November 10th letter came from a different world. She let us know that a photo of the three of us was in the *Tatler*. Undoubtedly a favor from one of her admirers—one couldn't help but marvel at her successes.

In our junior year we took a train to New England to visit our top three college choices, Wellesley, Smith and Mt. Holyoke. We knew we had to separate, and decided one of us would go to Wellesley, and one to Smith. Mt. Holyoke was thrown in as back up.

It didn't turn out to be that simple. Wellesley was deserted, due to the Harvard-Yale game, but the Smith campus was lively, due to an international fair. Mt. Holyoke was boring. Smith came out as the clear winner, posing a dilemma. Which of us would go to Smith, and which would be relegated to the second place Wellesley? The solution was obvious: we would both go to Smith, but request separate dorms.

Senior year I was elected Head of Student Government and Susan became editor of the Senior Year Book. One of my new jobs was to say grace in the cafeteria: "Bless this food to our use and this our school to thy loving service. Amen."

Everyone in our class was an atheist except for Ruth Farley, and we talked her out of God before graduation.

We were on top of the world; we had everything. Money was not an issue, and we could do it all: theater, opera, and museums with friends, Village jazz clubs with our dates.

If everything was so great why was I so hungry? The refrigerator was always there. The chocolate mousse, the left over goulash, the creamed spinach, the thought of it all was too much to bear. One bite and I was doomed, because one bite was never enough. Starvation was the easiest solution to the hunger.

Smith notified us we were assigned to the same dorm, Morrow House.

I looked forward to getting away from the refrigerator.

SMITH COLLEGE

*C*ollege in the '50s: Forget Jane Fonda, Princess Di, and the latest TV *special on Eating Disorders. Imagine a time when nobody ever heard of anorexia, let alone bulimia, gays were in the closet, and alcoholism was the only socially acceptable problem. Drugs? You're kidding. Being late for dinner was the worst thing we could do to our families. Eisenhower was in office. McCarthy was in the background. We were "the silent generation," and we did not make trouble.*

Social landscape: Clairol's ad slogan was "Does she or doesn't she? Only her hairdresser knows for sure." We did not "go all the way." We all dressed alike, did our homework, smoked like chimneys, drank hard liquor, and made sure we had a date on Saturday night. Everyone worried about weight, but not about food. Vegetarians and cholesterol did not exist. On dates we discussed poetry, not politics. Nobody was in therapy and nobody dropped out of college. In short, we were insufferable snobs, incredibly self-centered, and, above all, conformists.

Sue McLean, my roommate, pretty much summed up the mood of our time when composing a song for her senior class party. The theme of the party, "Manhattan" inspired these opening lyrics:

> *Because it tends to fatten*
> *When you're mixing my Manhattan*
> *Please eliminate the cherry and vermouth*
> *I don't want to sound suburban*
> *But to ruin bonded bourbon*
> *Seems to me to be outrageously uncouth.*

We arrived at Morrow House in 1953, along with a variety of entering Freshmen, from the quiet Southern belle, Nancy Franklin, to the noisy cheerleader-type, Wendy Nordstrom, with country-clubby Emily, Betsy, Karen, all blond, all clear-skinned, all skinny, amid screams of delight and side-long assessments. We looked each other over, while the housemother, Mrs. Proctor, served coffee in the living room. There were a couple of losers, but for the most part we were a scary group of winners.

The first days at Smith were a maze of activities. There was an orientation lecture for Freshmen in Greene Hall, during which it was explained we'd be given more work than we could handle, and we'd have to learn what to drop in order to get by; we were told not to drink because we were below the legal drinking age, but advised not to mix our drinks if we did; we were cautioned about obeying dormitory rules, and we were congratulated for being who we were, and wished good luck.

Who we were: We were smart, we were rich, we wore Bermuda shorts, knee socks, trench coats, and cardigan sweaters buttoned in the back. Our hair was cut shoulder length and, for the most part, hung straight. We knew we had it all.

Who we were: Not twins, but Marian and Susan, each going our own way.

I was surprised I had a name and people knew it. Marian? Marian Who? Me?

Susan somehow knew where she was going; I was always lost. Everyone else knew where to go to sign up for classes, and which classes to sign up for. Everyone else was smart and skinny and laughed easily. I pretended to be like every one else.

Why did I eat dessert? I feel fat. I'll make up for it and skip dinner.

We managed to separate so much that one of our dorm mates, Valerie Lamb, was shocked when she saw us together. "Oh my God, there are two of you. I can't believe it. I always wondered how you got around so fast." Everyone laughed.

We made separate friends. Susan's roommate, Suzanne Ruelland, was tall, elegant, French, and serious about Poetry. My roommate, Sue McLean, was blond, impatient, and not serious about anything. Sue was a talented musician and a standout at Morrow House for her popularity with men. Whenever the dorm phone rang someone screamed: "Sue, phone call!"

Sue could eat anything without worrying about it.

At the end of the day Sue and I joked about the others and our classes. We mimicked the Art 11 Professor's repetition of "the rhythmic repetition of the forms," and laughed about Professor Patch's admonition regarding exams: "of course I want you to parrot back what I give you in class." Patch's Chaucer classes were intense, and the homework was so voluminous he was surprised we did it: "When I taught at Yale they balked. The men wouldn't do it. Whereas you," he said, with a mixture of contempt and admiration, "will do whatever I give you." He had us read, in Middle English, the love letters fourteenth century nuns wrote to Christ.

Nancy Franklin, on our floor, is getting chubby. She's stopped coming down for meals and is on an egg and prune diet. Does it work?

As an English Lit major, I read. And read. And read. I read poetry: "No man is an island entire of itself," "Miniver Cheevy, child of scorn, grew lean as he assailed the seasons," "A poem should be palpable and mute, as a globed fruit," "He's dead. The old dog won't have to sleep on his potatoes any more to keep them from freezing," "Shall I part my hair behind? Do I dare to eat a peach?" " He wept that he was ever born, and he had reasons."

She says if you just eat eggs and prunes you lose your appetite.

I read novels: Henry Fielding, Thomas Hardy, Nathaniel Hawthorne, Henry James, Joseph Conrad, James Joyce, D.H. Lawrence, William Faulkner, Thomas Mann...and so on.

In class a hapless sophomore asked Miss Kalman why Thomas Mann used such complexity in one of his images.

"Because," Miss Kalman responded, "Thomas Mann didn't realize he was writing for an idiot reader."

THEY ALWAYS LEAVE DESSERT out in the kitchen after dinner, as a late night snack.

Russian Drama: "Why do you wear black, Masha? 'Because I am in mourning for my life,'"

"I am a tedious passing face...everywhere I was merely a passing face," "what still enthralls me is beauty. I am not indifferent to it," "a passing face...in mourning for my life... beauty..."

Tonight they left out strawberry shortcake. Strawberries, whipped cream, lots of helpings. Is anyone eating it? How can they stop after one helping?

It started sophomore year. It all started with Anna Whitman's seemingly brilliant suggestion: "Let's go to Green Street, binge on hot fudge sundaes, then get rid of them, Roman style, by vomiting them up." What a lark. What could be more satisfying than a guiltless gorge? Thanks, Anna! Why hadn't this occurred to me?

A group of us took off for the coffee shop, where we settled down to some serious eating and hilarity. Why stop? "The more you eat, the easier it will be to bring it up." After the coffee shop we headed to the corner market for some bags of cookies. Back to the dormitory, and the lavatory stalls. Anna was right; everything came up very easily. All it took was bending over, finger down the throat, up it came, no problem. Thank you, Anna.

Anna and I hit the Green Street coffee shop together now and then. The others lost interest. *How could they just forget about it and stop?*

Writing a paper on the irony in Eliot's *Portrait of a Lady*...trying to concentrate, writing, writing:

> "The epigram produces a distinct ironic contrast when set against the tone of the poem itself... 'Thou hast committed fornication: but that was in another country, And besides, the wench is dead'..."

There's bound to be some of that cobbler downstairs.

"Let us take the air, in a tobacco trance, Admire the monuments..." If I just concentrate on this paper I'll finish it tonight... "The ensuing effect is one of discord..."

I feel hot, then cold, and then I'm downstairs eating what's left of the cobbler. There must be something else down here; I need more, or I won't be able to bring it up. It's getting harder and harder to bring it up, and I need more. Is there any bread or cereal anywhere? It's too late to hit the coffee shop.

Back upstairs I wait until I'm alone in the lavatory. I tie my hair back, shove my finger down my throat. Panic. It's not coming up. Try again. Drink some water and try harder. At last, success. It's late. I'll finish the paper tomorrow, and if I skip meals I'll look okay for my date on Friday night.

The prospect of a weekend date made it easier to forego food. Instead of heading to the dorm, I'd write my papers in the coffee shop, skipping meals, stoking up on coffee and tomato juice. As for snaring men, if my skirt felt loose and my eyes weren't puffy, sitting back and looking interesting was not a problem, and it always worked. I needed men; it took a man to take my appetite away, and now and then we'd even hit it off and have a good time.

HARRY NESBITT WAS TALL and lean, with intelligent eyes and a dry sense of humor. He always got the joke, and we looked good together.

"Do you ever," he said, picking me up to drive me to Wesleyan, "do you ever dry clean that dress in between our dates?" It was my favorite slinky blue strapless; he'd seen it a hundred times; I knew I looked great so I laughed. Weekends at Wesleyan were terrific. I always returned happy and five pounds thinner.

Someone fixed me up with Ronnie Johnson, a blond crew cut from Yale and upstate New York. Ronnie was polite, he was serious, he was utterly boring. We had nothing in common and nothing to say to each other. At one point he mentioned his fraternity didn't accept Jews, because its policy was to recruit guys whose families would feel comfortable with each other. He himself had nothing against Jews, but he thought it was a sensible policy.

Should I have said "I'm Jewish"? No, because I really wasn't. The Jewish girls on campus hung out together.

What was I? A fraud.

Ronnie called for another date. How could he have enjoyed the first one? I was amazed. I considered telling him that I was Jewish and he'd hurt my feelings, but that would have been a lie on both counts. Besides, I didn't want to upset him; he was, basically, a nice guy. I gave him a believable excuse.

The best way to stay away from food was to line up the men. A weekend at Yale was fabulous, good for a great time and a guaranteed weight loss of at least five pounds.

Hamilton College, where Frankie (whoops, he was now Frank) went, was another favorite getaway, a little weirder than Yale, but interesting in its own right. Even more interesting: Frank was now dating my roommate, Sue. At some point I'd arranged a blind date, never dreaming it would work out. Miss Popularity with my self-conscious brother? Though, to be fair, I could see why girls would be interested: he had a kind of intense Gregory Peck look, an interesting attitude, and an unusual intellect. Yet it was hard to believe: Sue was in love with Frankie, whoops, Frank. Who would have thought it possible?

In our sophomore year Susan contracted mononucleosis, and had to lighten her course load. Her credits would have to be made up in the summer, and we decided to go to Harvard Summer School. Together. It was the summer of 1955; Harvard Square was teeming with Summer School students, and the banks of the Charles were lined with sunbathers.

Great! Sunbathing was the best way to forget food. It was a double-barreled cure-all, offering a suntan and a loss of appetite. Tanned and skinny! This was going to be a great summer.

WE SIGNED UP FOR Guerard's course on the American Novel—and, for kicks, intermediate French—a breeze, after Barnard's advanced French. Our rooms were in Wigglesworth, which bordered Mass. Ave. at one end of Harvard Yard, a stone's throw from the Crimson Shop, a couple of blocks from the Coop, and not far from the Brattle Theater and the Club Casablanca.

It was also directly across from an all-night cafeteria, but this would not be a problem. I wasn't hungry! There were lots of men around, a few of them really interesting.

Meals were cafeteria style in the big dining hall. It was easy to put very little on your tray and not go back for more—no sitting at family style dinners, as we did at Morrow House, staring at platters of food and waiting politely—here we could eat and run. This was going to be a great summer. I felt light and in control.

We were reading The Sun Also Rises. I envied Lady Brett, but identified with Cohen.

Susan was going with Ted Crowe, whom I had my eye on. Graduated with top honors in English Lit from Yale, very quiet, a little scary, a challenge. Good for Susan. We all went to an outdoor concert at the Hatch Shell on the Boston Esplanade. I was bored and folded my program into a high-flying paper airplane. Ted laughed. At the end of the concert Susan pulled me aside.

"Do you want him?"

"What?"

"He's too quiet for me, and you amuse him more than I do. Do you want him? I really don't mind."

"Honest?"

"Honest."

"This is crazy, but sure."

Now it was Marian, not Susan, going with Ted Crowe. He was brilliant, but too sensitive. One night when we were having drinks at the Casablanca we started discussing art and ethics. I disagreed that a great work of art had to have moral integrity. He changed the subject. I broke up with him the following fall...he would have seen through me soon enough.

❀ ❀ ❀

BACK TO THE MORROW House routine: the books, the papers, the exams, the weekends at Yale, the strawberry shortcake.

Just before my Music 11 exam I got a call from home: Omi was dead. An overdose of sleeping pills; Opi couldn't wake her in the morning.

Omi, angry and upset, not knowing what to do with her crochet hooks, holding up an egg and asking, "what do you call this?"

We went home for the funeral; I failed my Music exam.

It was getting harder and harder to vomit everything up. My puffy eyes were a dead giveaway, but nobody knew of what.

❊ ❊ ❊

MRS. PROCTOR WAVED THE telegram at me.

"Marian, your roommate has married your brother!"

So they'd gone and done it! They'd eloped! Sue had a year to go at Smith, and Frank was at Princeton, at the Woodrow Wilson School. They couldn't live together, but they were hitched. I was happy and worried at the same time. Sue was beautiful and talented, but she knew it, and she made sure everyone else did too. Did Frank know what he was getting into?

I pictured Mommy on the couch with her solitaire, and Daddy, listening to Richard Strauss. Left out of everything.

And then finally, drum roll: Graduation, the happiest day of my life! Nothing could top the exhilaration, not even the zombies we drank at Rahar's. No more grief! Nothing but smooth sailing ahead

No more grief, no more deadlines, no more bingeing, no more hunger! I knew I could do it; I could turn over a new leaf and be just like everyone else.

Publishing Procedures

First step? What every English Lit major went for: a Job in Publishing—whatever that meant.

Preparation: The Radcliffe Publishing Procedures Course, the summer program designed to clue us into the world of paste-ups, editing, production and design. We had rooms at Currier House, and lectures given by authors, editors, readers, publicists and every known variety of literary middlemen. I tried to pay attention, though my mind was on Clark Blum, my summer romance, and, of course, my weight

So far, so good. I was starving more than bingeing, and managing to stay the course.

I'd met Clark at a Currier House mixer, involving the usual chatter.

"Where? Oh, did you take his course in... do you know...class of '55... *blah blah...ha ha.*"

Clark caught my eye; he looked a little older, a little more amused than the rest. He was slightly overweight, with sandy colored hair and glasses. He came over, and we chatted about what we knew and where we were from. We began dating.

Clark had many talents—he painted, he wrote poetry, he was a scholar—and he was a boring engineer who worked at Raytheon. I detected a slight trace of a German accent; it turned out his parents were German refugees who had come to this country just about when we did. The accent was sad, somehow reminding me of my mother's game of solitaire.

We talked and talked. We talked about his friend Siri Rice, who was dating her psychoanalyst. Siri was beautiful and wild, a true Lady Brett; I envied her. We talked about the movie playing in the Square, *The Misfits,* starring Monroe and Gable.

"Just good enough to be depressing," Clark said. "No one's writing tragedy these days. Just pathos." … Gone, the noble downfall due to fate or flaw. Just the pathetic, the pitiable, the depressing...

We not only slept together, we became friends. Guilt about sex? Hell, no. Sex was part of the package, and decreased my appetite. Guilt about sex? I had bigger problems.

Clark showed me his translations of German poetry into English:

> "…ein wind soll kommen, und den kronen ausraufen ihr grunes gedachtnis…"

> "…let a wind come, and denude the crowns of their green memory…"

WIND —

We're on a sailboat, somewhere off the coast of Cape Cod. Siri and her psychoanalyst/lover are on deck, her blond hair newly dyed red, her Lady Brett mouth down-turned, eyes slits.

Angry at him? Us? Her life?

He's smirking his smart-ass analyst smirk. He'll probably tell her why she's angry. The jerk.

Clark at the mast, fooling with the sail. Clear skies, sea smell, slight breeze. Siri dives into the sea. Angry dive, graceful crawl, red head shrinking in the blue. "Don't worry, she's not going far," her shrink says.

Siri circles back, soundless ripples, slight foam.

He throws her a towel.

"How's the water?"

"Cold."

So is he.

Clark's still fooling with the sail.

The water's changing color, less appealing. Deeper. Please let's head back.

It's dark. Clark and I are back on shore, looking for a room. Siri and shrink have left us, thank God. They'll see us later—hopefully much later.

It's getting cold.

White cottage, 'Vacancy' sign. Old lady in the entry, standing at a desk.

"We'd like a room."

The woman grabs my left hand. Fingers bare.

"No rooms available." Angry smirk.

"Now I know what it feels like to be colored," Clark says on the way out.

The hell he does.

Next place I'll stand back, hands out of sight.

We get a room.

Why was I still so hungry? I was dying to eat, not another bite, but everything: bread, cake, steak, it didn't matter—followed by the panic and the lavatory and the vomit—the exhaustion and the puffy eyes. And the guilt.

And then the summer was over. It was time to tackle the next step up the ladder of Doing the Right Thing: Getting a Job in Publishing. Susan decided to stay in Cambridge, while I headed back to New York to get my act together. Pretending to be like everyone else was hard work.

TIDE

New York. I'd miss Clark, but he promised he'd visit. The important thing, until I could get away from home, was to stay calm, forget about the Barton's chocolates, the endless discussions about food, the pointless worries. "You're too thin, Marian, have some dessert." They saddened me, but I loved them. I had to get away.

In the *NY Times* Classified Want Ads:

"Editorial Assistant" at *Tide Magazine*.

Tide Magazine, the advertising trade journal? I'd written a paper on *Tide* at Radcliffe. The job was not appealing, but what the hell, here was a great opportunity to practice interviewing. Wear a suit, look good, sound like you know what you're doing.

Pretend.

Midtown Manhattan, not a bad location. Elevator to the seventh floor and into a small office. Several rooms, cluttered desks, an older woman smiling, and some guys with rolled up shirtsleeves. A scene from some movie everyone's seen. I was playing the part of a job applicant. This would be easy.

A youngish guy, Ken Something, looked over my resume and the Radcliffe paper.

"Very impressive," he said, "but this job is just for a research assistant... I'm not sure whether.."

Probably in his early thirties, smart-alecky face, frazzled manner, New York accent. Not bad.

"I need a job," I lied. "And this seems right for me." I smiled a winning smile. We continued the interview, each asking the appropriate questions.

"I'll let you know tomorrow."

I knew I had the job.

The job at Tide was right up my alley: my duties were mindless, but the people surrounding me weren't.

The older lady was Harriet, a wrinkled and friendly secretary, who told me about her AA meetings and showed me around, explaining my miniscule duties: "Before routing, dear, separate the mail into piles. If it looks like a story idea, send it to Ken, if it's an invoice, Neil gets it, the letters, the drafts go to Naomi, toss the junk mail, and any questions, ask me."

Ken was Ken Black, the managing editor. Neil Butler was sort of a boy Friday. Naomi Klein, an associate editor, was reasonably attractive, slightly overweight, and obviously brainy. She sat at her desk churning out articles, occasionally chuckling, about, presumably, her own wit. Ken and Naomi seemed very close; they often left the office together. There were some other guys with unknown duties in a back office.

So far, so good. I had the right kind of job; now I needed an apartment. I had to get away from home, from the couch, the refrigerator, the rolls from Gideon's Bakery.

Next stop: the Smith Club bulletin board. Several listings, but the standout was a bull's eye:

> Roommate wanted. Two bedroom apartment, W. 57th St. at 7th Ave., Tel. EN7-4414; after 5 PM, DD Maynard, Wellesley '56.

I loved 57th! Near Carnegie Hall, the Russian Tea Room, the galleries, the action.

The apartment turned out to be in a shabby building over a drugstore on the street floor. Great, perfect! Easy access to shampoo and aspirin. DD buzzed me in, and I walked up a flight of stairs.

"Hi, I'm DD! Come in and look around!" Short, blond pageboy, pug nose, familiar looking, undoubtedly easy to get along with. We checked each other out, chatting about our colleges, jobs, who we might know in common, and finally, the rent and her routine. The rent was no problem, the routine was even better: we'd share the cleaning and household expenses but each buy our own food, eat separately or together, whatever worked. She hesitated.

"My fiancé, Chris Carroll, sometimes sleeps over."

"Great," I said, "no problem." Thinking *whew*, she's not as goody-goody as she looks. We both smiled. It was a done deal.

Why couldn't I be like DD? Carefree, capable, uncomplicated. She cleaned, she shopped, she cooked and ate her dinner carelessly—food was not an issue. Where had I gone wrong? I watched her with wonder; she had no idea how much I envied her.

Why was I so hungry when everything was going so well? Coming home from work I passed the grocery, the fancy bakery, the corner restaurant and coffee shop. I walked quickly, eyes ahead, trying to think thin. One mistake, one wrong move, and I was in trouble. One wrong bite and there was no turning back from the panic of ice cream, cake, bread, it didn't even matter—whatever it took to bring it all back up.

DD posed a problem. I tried sneaking the bags of groceries into my bedroom, closing the door, and waiting until the coast was clear and she was out of the bathroom. Timing was important to get the job done right, and sometimes it was a long wait; DD liked to stay up late, reading, talking to Chris, putting her hair up in rollers.

Why can't I be like DD? Whatever it takes, I'll do it. I'll start tomorrow: think thin, think normal, think about books, think about men, think about Ken.

In the mirror the next morning I stared at puffy eyes and weighed myself.

Pretend it doesn't matter. Pretend you're DD.

Breezing into the office, big smile on my face. Harriet grinning over her typewriter, Ken racing around, Naomi glued to her story line.

Good morning, everybody. I'm no crazier than you are, and from now on, I'll prove it.

I WAS GETTING TO like them more and more, and I sensed it was mutual. I began to be included in weekly staff meetings, where we all pitched ideas: the turnover at BBD&O, gas station logos, the secretary who came up with "you'll wonder where the yellow went, when you brush your teeth with Pepsodent," the latest market research on candy versus chocolate—the ideas were rapid-fire and seemingly endless. I began joining their alcoholic lunches. It was easy to skip food at lunch; martinis were an acceptable substitute.

My job was getting to be fun. I learned, when calling for information, that if I said "Tide" in a certain way, the person on the other end would hear "Time," and do whatever it took to get me the info I needed. Ken and Naomi were paying more attention to me, and Ken started giving me more to do. He gave me some plum assignments, sending me to promotional parties launched by Hertz or Palmolive or Schlitz—it didn't matter—no need to write a story unless there was one, and there were always free drinks and attractive people. I felt like an attractive person, drink in hand, pretending to know what I was doing. Sometimes the feeling lasted through the night.

Naomi loosened up, tearing herself away from her desk now and then to join me at mine. I liked the warm laugh that matched her eyes. A Radcliffe grad, she was reading Proust and Gide in French. I picked up *Remembrance of Things Past*, and Gide's *Strait is the Gate*. Proust put me to sleep. Gide resonated.

> "Abel caught hold of my arm and dragged me out of doors into the night, and there we walked on and on for a long time without purpose, without courage, without reflection."

Think about something else. Think about tomorrow. Think about Ken— he's starting to show interest.

Some days were better than others; the nights were awful. No matter how hard I tried, the hunger got in the way. Nothing mattered—not DD, not Ken, not the latest movie—Gide, Proust, a phone call from Clark— nothing mattered but the corner bakery.

I had to get away, but where?

Oh no…don't do it…You'll just upset them.

I hailed a cab and took it home, to Mommy and Daddy and the living room couch.

How could I be so stupid? Now they know something's wrong, and all I'm doing is upsetting them.

"Marian, you're too skinny."

"What's wrong, Marian? You can tell us."

What's wrong? Where to begin? Your daughter is so hungry she has to throw up what she eats or else she'd be a circus attraction.

What's wrong? Nothing, except that my world revolves around food, and not much else. Ever hear of anything like it? Of course not.

I'm really sorry because I love you.

"Nothing's wrong. I'm just tired. Really. I'll try and get more sleep."

They didn't buy it, and scheduled an appointment for me with Doctor Hecht, a psychologist friend of theirs. I'd met Doctor Hecht on occasion, and remembered him as an intense guy with a nervous tic of a smile and an Austrian accent. He was reputedly a brilliant scholar and a brainy penetrator of the human psyche. He couldn't possibly understand; no one could, but I looked forward to the appointment. I was finally Doing Something, I was engaging in <u>Treatment Plan Number One</u>.

DOCTOR HECHT'S OFFICE WAS in his apartment, in a building not far from where I lived. The appointment was at 5:30, after work, and the streets were dark. I took the elevator to the sixth floor and rang the bell. Apartment 6-J.

"Please come in." Mrs. Hecht opened the door. Serious looking, no makeup, hair in a bun. Doctor Hecht appeared and shook my hand, nodding in a European way that reminded me of my parents. Grinning his weird grin, he led me to his office. The room, just off the central living area, was undoubtedly designed to be a family room or den. Doctor Hecht sat at a huge desk, and I sat across from him in a stiff-backed chair. We were surrounded by an incredible number of books for a room of this size; it was awe-inspiring.

"Your parents are worried about you. Are they right? Can you tell me about it?"

He was staring at me with his intense gaze. Could he help me? Not a chance. I felt like crying. There was no way I could tell him about "it."

"I'm going through kind of a hard time at work, and I get more upset than I should about a lot of things. I have trouble sleeping. I'll eat too much and then make up for it by not eating at all." I tried my winning smile. "They're worried because they think I'm crazier than I am, which is pretty bad."

He wasn't grinning.

"I think we have some work to do. What do you think?"

I think about food, and I think I have nowhere else to turn.

"I think you're right."

That was the beginning, and "some work" continued with Doctor Hecht on a weekly basis. He gave me a battery of tests: Rorschach, Stanford-Binet, the Thematic Apperception Test. He was an expert in handwriting analysis; he tested my handwriting. His specialty was physiognomy; he tested my ability to read faces. These were all interesting and harmless exercises. Doctor Hecht's conclusions were all—surprise, surprise—an attempt at ego boosting: I had many talents, a high IQ, excellent insights and a solid academic background. I was, according to him, a roaring success, and all I needed was to build up my self-esteem.

Well, you've missed the boat this time, Doctor. I'm a failure. And when I get home I'm probably going to eat and throw up to prove it.

In the several sessions that followed we discussed my reading.

"*The New Yorker* is too frivolous for you...I have a book that you should try."

My parents: "Charming and cultivated, I like them very much, but intellectual snobs...turning down their noses at sports and popular entertainment...very difficult for you."

Wrong again: Narrow-minded in many ways, but not in the important ones. Maybe they don't understand baseball or The Hit Parade, but they put up with me.

I dutifully started reading Jung's *Introduction to Psychology*, and found him interesting but silly, with his theories of the collective unconscious, archetypal patterns and types. I cleverly typed Jung, according to his own definitions, as an Introverted Thinking Type. Of course he didn't have a category for me—who could possibly imagine such a thing?

My weekly sessions with Doctor Hecht continued, and became a pleasant routine. Though they weren't particularly helpful, he was a nice man who lent me books and seemed to care. I didn't talk to him about the eating.

WORK AT *TIDE* CONTINUED at a smooth pace until, one morning, Ken called me into his office. *Uh-oh.* Morgan Brown, the editor in chief, who rarely made an appearance, had come and gone, leaving Ken, Naomi and Neil sitting together.

Bloody Hell. What now?

"Sit down, Marian."

Okay, let's get it over with.

"Now that you've been here for a couple of months, we think it's time for you to move on up. We'd like to offer you an editorial position." They all looked at me expectantly, smiling warmly.

Good grief. What do I do now? I'm fine where I am; no need to rock the boat with deadlines and bylines and drafts and re-drafts. Eeeek!

"Gee! I really appreciate it. I love working here and I love you all. Thanks!"

What have I done? Why couldn't I have said, "I'll think about it,"? Why? Because, that would have been totally ungrateful. What do I do now? Let me out of here. I'm hungry.

As I was leaving, Ken grabbed his coat and followed me to the elevator. "Join me for a drink?"

"Sure."

This is it! I knew he was interested!

We walked to Napoli's, and sat at a table in their bar area.

"What's the problem?"

HUNGER — A MEMOIR

"The offer is great, and I don't want to seem ungrateful, but it would be too much for me right now."

"What's the problem?"

Uh-oh! Think fast. Make it good.

"Well, I just went through a nasty break up, and I've been feeling pretty down. I can't handle more responsibility right now. Routine clerical works fine."

Whew. He's looking sympathetic.

"Look, you should have said something. We're all friends here, you know."

"Sorry! You all took me by surprise, and I didn't want to seem ungrateful."

Our drinks came. The usual: martinis. He grabbed a handful of nuts and tossed them in his mouth. I wasn't even hungry.

"Well, if you like routine clerical, you'll get routine clerical. Kind of a waste, but we aim to please." He smiled, and I smiled back.

Enormous relief. More than relief. I've done it!

The waiter brought another round.

"Hungry?"

"No, but I'll join you."

I ordered another drink and he ordered spaghetti.

"Are you sure you won't have something?" He smiled. "You sure toss them down," said as a compliment.

"No thanks, I'll eat later," I lied.

Eureka. I've snared the big fish, the one I'd hoped for.

I watched him eat his spaghetti. Magic: I wasn't hungry.

That was the beginning of my Ken Black saga. He thought it best to keep our relationship a secret at the office, so we headed separately for the elevator. (Naomi told me later that this routine, rather than fooling anybody, was a source of general hilarity.)

Ken lived at Waverley Place, in an apartment he shared with his mostly absent roommate, Bob LaRue. The location, in the heart of the Village at Washington Square, was perfect. We'd stroll through the Square to our favorite haunts: the The White Horse Tavern, Rienzi's, and the Aurore, a little Italian restaurant where he ate and I drank.

Martinis, daiquiris, straight bourbon, it doesn't matter—he's amazed at how much I can belt down without getting sick—he should only know what it takes to make me sick.

Ken was different from my erstwhile ivy leaguers; he was down to earth, and had a cynical New York sense of humor I'd grown up with and almost forgotten. We had fun together, and the days passed for me without the usual *sturm und drang.*

Of course we had sex. It was good, not great, and didn't matter that much. What mattered most was easing the hunger, and that was happening. I was very grateful.

We decided to get engaged.

He decided, and I went along.

We'd announce our engagement at a big New Year's Eve party, at his Waverley Square apartment. It was a perfect party place: great location, big living room, piano, not much furniture. Bob LaRue on the piano. We made a list, and I shopped around and found the perfect dress, a backless black velvet.

I'm skinny, slinky, looking good, feeling like—what's the name of the girl in I Am A Camera? Feeling like that girl. Black backless, next to the piano, drink in hand, background music—Sally Bowles—that's me.

It was Christmas, the best time to be in New York. Everybody shopping like crazy, stores beribboned and bedecked, Park Avenue transformed by white-lit evergreens, bells ringing, Christmas colors everywhere—laughter and parties all over the place.

Ken bought me a recording of Don Giovanni, my favorite opera. It was time to take him home to meet the parents.

Uh-oh.

Mommy and Daddy were very cordial. We sat down to dinner.

Something's wrong.

Sitting there, at the dining room table, Ken didn't look or sound the same.

I don't see Ken, I see a Damon Runyon character. My world is crashing to a halt. I'm scared and I'm hungry.

Ken left to go home. I stayed.

In the morning Daddy came into my bedroom. He looked out the window.

"You're not marrying him, are you?"

"No."

"We didn't think you were serious."

I'm not serious, I'm hungry.

The problem is Ken's serious. The problem is we're planning to announce our engagement at a New Year's Eve party. The problem is we're giving the party, everyone's invited...what have I gotten myself into? What have I gotten him into?

"I don't want to hurt his feelings."

I didn't have to tell him it was over. He knew. We threw the party anyway. I wore my black backless dress and Bob LaRue played the piano. The party was a roaring success.

I gave notice to *Tide*, and left shortly after they found my replacement, a dopey blond who was undoubtedly right for the job.

Cambridge, Again

New York was over. I was heading back to Cambridge.

Away from parents and doctors and fiancés, back to tree lined streets, books, poetry, late night discussions over coffee…back to the comfort of the unknown.

I called Susan, who was working at Houghton Mifflin and lived near Harvard Square: great job, nice place.

How does she do it?

"Sure, why not come! You can stay with me until you get settled."

Settled? Settled where, how, and with whom?

"Great! Will it be okay with the others?"

Susan was living with a couple of social work students, Nancy Gray and Linda Mayberry. Of course they wouldn't mind.

"No problem. I'm not here most of the time anyway; I spend most nights with Ben."

How does she do it? Ben La Farge, a fellow editor at Houghton Mifflin, is the ultimate catch: incredibly handsome and civilized, good sense of humor, fun to be with…lucky Susan…good for her!

Chatting with DD as I packed my bags. Our lease was up, and she was going home to plan her wedding.

Everyone's engaged or married; even Susan and Ben are heading in that direction.

My only direction is to the refrigerator.

Try to smile. This will be a new beginning.

WHEN I ARRIVED AT 26D Shepard Street no one was home. A two-story yellow clapboard house in a great location: off Massachusetts Avenue, convenient to the MTA, and within walking distance of Harvard Square.

Evergood Market a few blocks away; A&P further away towards Porter Square.

The key was under the mat, as Susan said it would be. The living arrangement was standard graduate student: a living room cluttered with books, notes and records, a small dark kitchen, and the usual tiny upstairs bedrooms. Susan said everyone shared living expenses and household routines but bought their own food and liquor.

Food: Nothing interesting in the refrigerator—wait a minute—what's in the foil-covered dish? I better get out of here and stick to my starvation diet... this is a new beginning!

Nancy was the first to arrive.

"Hi, Marian! How was your trip? I guess you know the setup here, but any questions, ask me." Tall, lean blond, efficient manner, tight grin—Nancy was the designated director of the operation, taking care of the lease, the rent, and arguments with the landlord, Mr. Fink.

I'll bet that casserole is hers. Good thing I didn't take a bite. She'd notice.

"How about a drink?"

"Great. I'll drink from Susan's bottle—does she have one down here?"

"She's not around much anymore. Have some of my scotch."

Nancy put on a record and poured two drinks. I settled back on the couch with my scotch and lit a cigarette. Listening to Miles Davis...a far sight better than DD's show tunes.

Things are definitely looking up.

Nancy stretched her long legs and yawned. "Is Susan coming back here tonight?"

"Sure. At least as far as I know. She said she'd see me after work."

"Well, she hasn't been around much." Pause. She took another sip. "What do you think of her and Ben?"

I pictured Susan and Ben together. His handsome face, his funny smile, next to Susan with her big eyes and nice bone structure.

She's prettier than I am.

"You mean what do I think of them together? I love Ben. I think it's great."

Nancy yawned again. "It's looking pretty serious to me… it's looking like…well, they're really happy together."

Susan and Marian…Susan and Ben…Marian and…?

Linda Mayberry barged in with a shopping bag and lots of commotion. Medium height, slightly pudgy, big brown eyes, brown hair, fussy expression.

"Hi, Marian, great to see you. Sorry I can't stop and chat—I've got to unload this stuff and meet Brad—I'm late."

From the kitchen: "Susan coming home?" Cabinet doors opening and slamming shut.

"See you later!"

Gone.

Nancy poured herself another drink. I lit another cigarette. The plaintive strains of "Round Midnight" still in the air.

"Refill?"

"Sure, thanks."

This is my kind of place.

By the time Susan and Ben walked in, it was dark, Nancy was in the kitchen, and I was listening to an old Marlene Dietrich album.

Falling in love again, never wanted to, what am I to do, can't help it…

Susan grinned and Ben smiled.

"Hi, Marian…Oh, I love that thing from *The Blue Angel*…is it your record or mine?"

"It must be yours because it was here. Hi, Ben."

They sat across from me.

"Sorry we're late…it's all your sister's fault—but you know how she is, or, I should say, isn't, sticking to a schedule…"

Ben has a well bred speaking voice—old school, modulated, a touch of irony…

He got up. "It's late. Let's go somewhere close for dinner…how about the Midget?"

"Gee, thanks, but I had something to eat at the airport," I lied. "Go without me, I'll be fine. I have to unpack. Sure it's okay, Susan, that I'm in your room?"

"Sure. I won't be back tonight, but I'll see you tomorrow." Looking worried, "Are you okay? Do you need anything?"

Take off, have fun, and don't feel guilty about me. I'm fine, I'm great, I'm starting over, and this is the place to do it.

"I'm great!"

And I was great, for at least a month.

Just as everyone suspected, Susan was basically out of the picture at 26D, and I took her place. A smooth transition from one twin to the other, no need to do a roommate search on anyone's part, everyone happy.

Clark still lived close by and became a regular presence, but there were plenty of other men, and music in the background: Monteverdi, Billie Holiday, Charlie Parker, Vivaldi, whatever the mood called for, and the mood was good.

Eureka, I'm doing fine with food. In control, skipping meals, not even hungry. Losing weight in the bargain. Life has never been better.

Music and men, just what the doctor ordered.

Nancy's boyfriend, Dan Kavanaugh, was another regular, and his tall straightforward presence was a great antidote to Clark's sardonic wit. Dan was Harvard Law, Air Force Reserve, terrific looking, and refreshing. Problem: when they were together, Clark was at his worst, always trying, idiotically, to get the better of him in some irrelevant debate. It made me furious with Clark. What a jerk.

We all know you're brilliant, Clark, so please shut the hell up and leave the guy alone.

You'll never win, because he doesn't give a damn. And neither do I.

Here's how it happened: *You'll see it's not my fault.*

One night Dan offered to drive to the Square to pick up some booze.

"You want to come along, Marian?"

"Sure."

Why not? I'm not doing anything.

In the car Dan tells me he's really been hanging around 26D because of me, not Nancy. He's interested. How do I feel?

Great! Surprised...really surprised, but come to think of it, great!!

"What about Nancy?"

"We're not tied to each other, and the way things have been going, I think she'll understand."

He's right. Nobody's tied to anybody. Nobody's married, and it's all a game. Let's, please, just have fun.

Nancy didn't understand. She didn't talk to me. Neither did Linda, who was hardly ever around, and didn't matter.

Oh my God, she's crying in her room. Nancy, if it wasn't me, it would be someone else. It's all a matter of timing. I'm not to blame...am I? What did I do this time!

Dan and I started dating. He was too perfect: good looking, smart, impenetrable—what the hell did he see in me? I couldn't crack his code.

He's a total challenge. Different from the others—not in the least bit crazy. I can't believe he's real. What does he see in me?

Slowly, slowly, Nancy got over it. We began to talk.

Thank goodness, there are always men around, and she's interested in someone else.

Everything was back to normal. Next step in Doing the Right Thing: employment.

With my sterling journalistic credentials it was no problem getting a job. I landed up at the *Harvard Business School Magazine*, in a position that was so boring it did the unimaginable, it fanned a spark of ambition into a flame, and I actually decided to make a career move. Enough of advertising and corporate greed—I wanted to help others—and what better way than what my roommates were doing? The social work field was very appealing, with its exploration of the human psyche and its methodology to ease stress. The more I talked to Nancy the more I knew it was for me.

Getting in to the Simmons School of Social Work was not a problem. My interview with Dean Rutherford went smoothly. I would start classes in the fall.

It was spring, the best time in Cambridge. A general celebratory air at the end of the deep freeze, with people emerging into the outdoors as if they'd never been outside before, laughing, smiling, congratulating each other on the fine weather, forsaking, at long last, boots and snowsuits for short sleeves and sweaters.

"Skip the MTA, let's walk to the Brattle and see what's playing…"

Tennis rackets, windows open, birds, buds, you name it, it's finally spring.

So why am I spiralling downhill again? There's nothing wrong, there's nothing wrong, there's nothing wrong…except me.

Everything was going great. I was living in the best place with simpatico roommates. I had plenty of friends, lots of men, a graduate program that suited me perfectly—hell, I was even skinnier than ever.

Nothing to blame and nowhere to turn. Running away and running around, from the Evergood to the Greek diner to the two-bit corner deli up the street, hiding bags of chips and cheese, waiting, waiting, until the coast is clear and I can use the bathroom. Panic: If I wait any longer I won't be able to bring it all up. At long last! Finally, it's time to try and make it to bed before it's time to go to work.

I bumped into Linda on her way down to breakfast as I was heading up to bed. She gave me a cheery Good Morning, thinking, no doubt, that I'd had a more eventful night than she. Possibly even envying me. If she only knew! But how could she possibly know, or even imagine such a thing as me? Thank God, nobody could.

Who am I? A secret.

Fall. A frightening season; the party's over. No more gin and tonics on the balcony listening to Songs of the Auvergne, with the sound of laughter in the street. The nights are getting colder. The sounds of footsteps, once carefree, now purposeful and hurried. Car doors slam. It's time to get serious.

Uh-oh…

I started classes at Simmons. On the positive side, my classmates were, on the whole, a surprisingly good group. I made new friends: Sally Herman, Susan Dole, Kathy Weiss, all smart, articulate and funny. On the negative side, the course work was, on the whole, surprisingly disappointing. We studied Freud and took notes on the niceties of his three stages of development, Oral, Anal, Oedipal.

Yawn. Okay, I'm supposedly stuck in stage one. What of it? This stuff is hard to remember because it doesn't make sense, which means I'll have to study for the exam. Damn!

My first student placement was at the V.A. outpatient clinic on Court Street, in Scollay Square. The clinic was just past The Steaming Kettle, an oddball teashop with a huge gilt teapot hanging over its entrance, spewing steam and a powerful nicotine-coffee odor. That odor permeated the entire street; it was depressing, just like the work I had to do. My caseload consisted mostly of ex-GI's who needed medical coverage, a simple directive (i.e., try getting a job), or someone to talk to. They were all lonely.

There was one exception to my usual caseload: a paranoid schizophrenic, whose case was referred to me because I was "the least threatening." He stared at me with his scared and scary deep brown eyes and told me how "they were out to get him." He struck a chord. I tried to reassure him.

It's getting to be a nightly routine: the hunger, the shopping, the eating, the endless waiting for the coast to clear so I can get the job done and try and get some sleep.

November 1958 — Susan and Ben get married! A small Justice of the Peace ceremony, with Ben's brother Tim and me as witnesses. No drum roll, no throwing rice around. We all go to the Casablanca for a celebratory drink.

Susan is now Susan LaFarge. Forget Susan and Marian; it's now Susan and Ben LaFarge.

Great! I love Ben, and I'm really happy for Susan.

The nights are getting worse.

Returning home from work on the MTA, an old lady offered me her seat. "You look more tired than I feel, dear."

Good God, it's beginning to show.

Another day a passer-by stopped me on Mass. Ave.

"What's the matter, dear?"

"This is just my normal tragic expression, I'm fine." I flashed a smile.
The joke's over.

I needed to talk to someone. Not Susan—she was too close. Linda?
Out of the question. Maybe Nancy. Of course I couldn't mention the eating business, but I could say I was so tired and stressed I might need help.
She'd know what to do.

"I had the feeling something was wrong, Marian. You've got to get help, and I can tell you who to call." Nancy worked at the Massachusetts General Hospital. Within minutes she gave me the number of their Psychiatric Outpatient Clinic, and told me to ask for an appointment with a Doctor Semrad.

Doctor Semrad's looks and manner put me at ease, and I went as far as I ever had in opening up about myself. I even told him about the eating and vomiting.

"Can your parents afford the help you need?"

"Yes."

"Then you must get it. This is a clinic, but there are many top notch psychiatrists in the area who can help you." He jotted down some names and handed me a slip of paper.

"Will you call your parents?"

"Yes. Thank you for your help."

I stuck the paper in my pocket and left his office.

Thinking of Mommy's sad expression, Daddy's anxious pacing in the living room, Mahler in the background.

They're happy everything is going so well. How can I upset them?

The slip of paper disappeared. I didn't look for it.

There's no way anyone can help me. I can do it on my own.

I was spiraling downhill. The nights were the worst.

Trying to sleep. Remembering Heart of Darkness, Kurtz's "The horror, oh the horror." Remembering Bartleby's answer to the world, "I'd prefer not to." Thinking "the center will not hold." Thinking "we walked on and on for a long time without purpose, without courage, without reflection."

Trying to sleep. Thinking: The Horror, Oh The Horror.

I called home. Mommy and Daddy responded with a flurry of activity and phone calls, resulting in Treatment Plan Number Two.

DOCTOR MEYER'S OFFICE WAS on Beacon Street, near Coolidge Corner, Brookline. I decided to wear all black, in dramatic keeping with the circles under my eyes.

His office was on the first floor of a brownstone. I waited in a nondescript waiting room, until the door opened.

"Come in." He was tall, bald, and unexpectedly strong looking. I couldn't really tell—his name was noncommittal—but I guessed Jewish.

We walked in and sat at either end of the room, facing each other. Neither of us spoke.

Dead silence. His calm expression was, weirdly enough, both unsettling and reassuring.

I decided to enter the fray: "Well, I expect I'll begin."

Silence.

"You'll probably want to know why I'm here."

He shifted in his chair.

In desperation I told the truth.

"My problem is food. I don't have a normal appetite. I'm always hungry. I either starve or binge and vomit it all up. I vomit because I'm scared of getting fat; I can't stand the thought of fat. I'm hungry right now, and when I leave I'll probably eat and vomit."

Amazingly enough, he hasn't changed expression.

I heard myself going on and on, trying to recoup what was left of my dignity, trying to be interesting.

He never changed expression. Finally he spoke. "I think we can work together. It won't be easy, and it will take time to probe beneath a symptom such as yours, to find the underlying cause...are you willing?"

Am I willing? AM I WILLING? You mean there's hope? I'm willing to do WHATEVER IT TAKES! WHEN CAN WE START?

"Sure, if you're willing, so am I."

We arranged a schedule—once a week until he could fit more times into his schedule—he'd like to see me three times a week, if I was up to it. Standard fee: twenty-five dollars an hour. Could I handle it?

There's hope! THERE'S HOPE!

"Yes, sure. I'll do whatever it takes—I may have to cut some classes, but I can manage that—and you can bill my parents."

I gave him my father's address and phone number.

"Regarding the bill, I'm sure you understand, what goes on here is confidential. I'll send your father my bill, but I won't discuss our work together with your parents. Will that work out?"

Whatever it takes, whatever you say…I'LL DO ANYTHING, AND SO WILL THEY!

"Yes, I'm sure they'll understand. I'll let them know."

I soared out of his office and ran down Beacon Street to catch the MTA. It was cold, but I felt too good to hail a cab—there was no need, no panic—I was re-entering the human race, I was on my way! I wasn't even hungry.

Whatever happens, I'm on my way!

Feeling good, looking good. Dancing around the living room to Linda's dopey Frank Sinatra record. Music and men—lots of men and music—I dusted off my Sally Bowles routine—I was on my way!

A new favorite: Walker Rowan, who appeared with Ben and Susan one evening—intriguing and handsome—in fact he looked like Ben—a tidbit for Doctor Meyer. He was divorced, he was literate, he was right up my alley, and we started dating.

No more eating! Watch out, world, I'm on my way! Thank you, Doctor Meyer.

I saw Doctor Meyer once, twice, then three times a week. He stared at me as I talked and talked and talked—about Susan, about Frankie, about Daddy's temper, Mommy's passive nature, the war—about everything except the hunger.

How am I doing, Doctor? Do you find me amusing, interesting, witty, complicated?

One week, and then another. He continued to stare, and I continued to expound, hoping I was heading in the right direction. I wore black.

Black: "I am in mourning for my life" Get it, Doctor? Do you find me fascinating?

He stared and I talked, grasping at his prompts, following his cues, hoping I was doing okay, trying, trying to feel the right thing—but flunking.

Sure, my mother's passive, but I never longed for mothering. What's wrong with me? And as for feelings for my father, way back when? Way back when he was trying to get us the hell out of England during the Blitz? Sorry, Doc, no Oedipal longing, just sorrow.

What was I feeling? Fat.

I look like hell. Too fat to go out with Walker this weekend.

My classes at Simmons continued to be boring—in fact I stopped showing up for most of them. Exams were coming up. Freud was easy, methodology was basic common sense, statistics was the only problem—I'd have to borrow Sally's notes. The VA continued to be depressing. I dreaded walking by the teapot, especially in the cold.

They'll be eating dinner when I get home. Eating, laughing: Hi, Marian, join us...want some casserole, there's plenty...

Where was I going? Downhill.

In spite of the good doctor, in spite of the good effort, the good people—my God, I'm surrounded by good people—good this and good that—in spite of it all, I'm sliding, sliding, sliding...and there's no way up.

Men didn't help—in fact they were part of the problem—they were always around, there was always a party, the coast was never clear. One night, the worst: I'd binged big time, my stomach was so distended I could hardly breathe—there was no way to deal with it at home, and nowhere to go. I took a cab to Ben and Susan's.

"Marian, you can't do it here—oh my God—we have people over—where else can you go?"

Now I've got her all upset—and she's having a dinner party—good going, Marian, spread the misery around.

I cabbed back home, snuck upstairs, and waited, waited, until the coast was clear. It was a long wait.

"Doctor Meyer, I'm in real trouble. I really need help. I'm puking my brains out. I don't know what to do. What can I do?"

Don't cry, don't cry, don't cry.

Before I knew it, I landed up in Treatment Plan Number Three: McLean Hospital.

TREATMENT PLAN NUMBER THREE:
MCLEAN HOSPITAL

When I told Dean Rutherford I had to drop out of Simmons to enter McLean he couldn't believe it.

"You're doing so well here, Marian...are you sure? Your doctor recommends? Well I certainly want the best for you...I can't believe...well you don't appear..."

What he really means is, you don't appear to be crazy.

If I'm not crazy, what am I?

Mommy and Daddy appeared on the scene, rooms booked at the Commander.

Why can't we make them happy? First Frank elopes, then Susan leaves them out, now this—I've outdone everybody! Goddamn, they deserve better. Why can't we make them happy?

Suddenly we're all in a cab heading for Belmont, to McLean Hospital. It's only about a fifteen-minute ride. Very convenient for my friends to visit.

Daddy looks twitchy and nervous, Mommy looks sad. They feel sorry for me, but they shouldn't! This is going to be great—literally what the doctor ordered. No more veterans, no more casserole in the frig, no more panic—not at McLean, my Magic Mountain.

"What's the saying? Something like, 'Every Boston blueblood has a horse in the stable and an aunt at McLean.'" They're not amused. Poor Daddy, looking so grim.

The cab turns off Pleasant Street and continues up a hill, Mill Street, through an open gate, onto a path leading to a circular driveway. Great

Scot, this looks like a college campus! Rolling green lawns, academic look-ing buildings, a tennis court. A young nurse in uniform walks by.

The cab drops us off at the entrance to the central administration building. And then a flurry of activity: A social worker greets us, answers some questions, then takes us to meet Doctor Ball, who is, apparently, in charge of intake.

Nice looking, gray hair, English accent. So far, so good.

He explains he'll be doing the initial interviewing and testing, that af-ter I sign my 'voluntary papers' I'll be escorted to my room, while my parents, if they don't mind, answer some questions. "But you mustn't feel left out," turning to me, "you'll be answering questions as well." *Ha ha.* We laugh politely.

I sign myself in, and, right on schedule, a nurse appears. Is she the one we saw from the cab? It doesn't matter.

She tells me her name, "Mary," and gives me a professional smile. We walk down a long gray hall. Various shapes and sizes of women are either pacing the hall or staring at us vacantly.

The faces of the mentally ill.

Uh-oh.

My room: stark gray walls, a low wooden bureau, a bed, a closet. Mary is talking. "Smoking is allowed, of course, but no matches or lighter so you'll have to ask for a light…"

She thinks I'm crazy, She's talking, talking at me…I'll get my luggage to-morrow, after it's reconnoitered—no bottles, no sharp edges—no money or papers of identification—my pocket book is gone. She's still talking…

Mary, still at it, tells me my stay in this building will only be for two or three weeks, for my "orientation," or period of testing, "… you'll be taking lots of tests. Then they'll assign you to a different ward."

Whew…there's hope. I'll ace those tests, and I'm outta here. Meanwhile, this is an adventure. Take advantage of it; add it to your story line.

Story line? I'll keep a journal.

JOURNAL ENTRY: MARCH 10, Tuesday —

Arrived yesterday. Snow on ground, short trip. Mommy and Daddy sad and anxious. After a brief meeting with a social worker, and a Doctor Ball, they disappear. Gone. What's the saying—out of sight, out of mind? I hope it's true. A student nurse, treating me like a nut case, explained the prison rules. No this, no that, nothing sharp, no money. I guess a lot of loonies try to slit their wrists or run away. Worrisome setting, until she told me this was only temporary—after a couple of weeks of tests I'll be sprung from here and move to greener pastures. I hope. Of course I will.

Dinner in a small dismal dining room, with tables of various sizes. None of my fellow inmates looked promising, and nobody looked up when I walked in and sat at a table for four. Two of my dinner companions stared at their plates in mute dismay—the third had a lively expression, and I tried a warm smile. Her response, with a wink: 'You'd do better with a blond wig, dear, but I like your hair.'

After dinner I tried to find a semi-rational compatriot, but gave up after my talk with a girl who seemed totally in touch. She spoke coherently, asked where I lived, and answered questions relevantly—suddenly she walked to a wall and knocked her head against it rhythmically. 'This helps when I get nervous.'

Surprise: I wasn't hungry, and can't remember what I ate.

[From McLean Hospital Records]

Nurse's report, March 1959

Miss Seidner seemed to seek out the talkative and alert patients. She kept herself busy by going to O.T. and walking. She was very full of questions about the hospital, and sometimes rather demanding of the nurses, becoming upset when things could not be done as she wanted, such as going from place to place.

This isn't as bad as I thought it would be. There are things to do: O.T. (Occupational Therapy) is the best—an art studio for painting and ceramics—with an artist-instructor who's obviously, thank God, not a psychiatrist, nurse, or amateur psychologist. His name is Lars something, and he's not bad looking. Also, morning calisthenics in a gym, even golf lessons. And I've found patients who aren't total nut cases—things are definitely looking up. Martha Miller, about my age, says I look familiar—she's from Great Neck, dark hair, pretty—what's she doing here? I never saw her before...maybe she met Susan.

Problem: I don't have "ground privileges," which means I can't go outside without a nurse.

JOURNAL ENTRY: MARCH 14, Saturday —

An exasperated phone call from Clark Blum, who asked me how I managed to land myself up in a loony bin and said, 'you're not crazy. Get the hell out of there.'

Actually, I'm getting to enjoy some of my fellow loonies. This morning I breakfasted with Nan Morley, a Wellesley grad with bandaged wrists, and Mrs. Pond, a schizophrenic, unpredictable, but intelligent. We discussed the 'Ides of March'—I brought it up by mentioning tomorrow, March 15, is my brother's birthday. Mrs. Pond began discussing the origin of the phrase, when Nan interrupted.

"This conversation's too sane for this place. Let's have a little more insanity, please."

Ruthie, from the next table, as if on cue, shouting, top volume: "Will one of you pipsqueaks lemme outta here! Why such crap lives, when nice people like us can't, is beyond me!' Nan: ' That's more like it."

They took away my steel knitting needles and said they'd order plastic ones.

It's a beautiful morning with a hint of spring, the sun intensified by yesterday's snowfall. I managed, after strenuous nagging, to get a hike on the morning agenda, and three of us, accompanied by a nurse, spent an hour walking around the grounds. I had to stop myself from bursting into song—I knew the nurse would record it as some sort of a symptom of insanity. Am I guilty of the same—of misjudging the commonplace remarks of my fellow patients? It doesn't really matter.

[From McLean Hospital Records]

March 16, 1959

She talks with facility during interview and although her perceptions are very subjective, her speech and vocabulary are of such an order that they promote a great degree of credibility in the listener. Such distortions are in the nature of a subtle twist to actual accounts.

Signed, Robert E. Ball, M.D./cmg

I WALK DOWN THE hall to hear Ruthie Krauss, my favorite schizophrenic, play the piano.

Ruthie turns to me and winks, "This one's for you," she says, and plays 'Sweet and Lovely.'

Who?…Me? Uh-oh. I feel like I'm going to cry.

Remembering she's a fan of Perry Como, I remark, "All we need around here is Perry Como."

She winks again.

"He'll probably show up—everyone else does—why not? "

JOURNAL ENTRY: MARCH 20, Friday —

Manic-depressive Mrs. Kupfer just left my room, after delivering the following lecture:

"Yesterday you came in to look at my books, yet today you didn't come in and say how are you, Mrs. Kupfer? That just goes to show what happens when you're nice to people. You think you're someone just because you went to Smith and Simmons, or just because your parents have money, or I don't know. Well, I'll tell you, you're a dime a dozen, cutie, and just you wait. Just you wait until they give you sleeping pills and then take them away until you scream for sleep. Then they'll put you in Wyman Hall for depressed patients. Just wait until you get violent and tear your hair. Just wait. Try and get out of here and see what happens.'

Getting more and more agitated.

'There's no freedom of speech here.'

Me: 'There's never freedom of speech if you don't want to hurt people's feelings.'

Mrs. K.: 'Well I always say what I want, and my feelings have been hurt plenty of times.'

Departure.

❀ ❀ ❀

DOCTORS, DOCTORS, TESTS AND more tests and more doctors: Doctor Haecox, Doctor Rice, Doctor Ball, Doctor Pierce, and of course, good old Doctor Meyer, twice a week.

The Rorschach, TAT, SCT, DAP — How am I doing, everybody?

[From McLean Hospital Records]

Seidner, Marian #19354 (Admitted: March 9, 1959)

CASE HISTORY

ORIENTATION:

Identifying Data: The patient was examined on March 9, 1959 in the admission unit. She is Miss Marian Seidner, a 24 year old, white, single woman who is a Social Work student at Simmons College...support is derived mainly from her parents...

Admission Data: She was admitted March 9th and at the time of the examination stated it is her first admission to a psychiatric hospital. She had been receiving psychotherapy from Doctor Meyer for a period of four to five weeks at a period of three times a week and he had referred her to this hospital. She was accompanied by her parents on her arrival and signed a voluntary paper. She was admitted to ABII ward. Financial competence is said by the parents to be adequate.

Affective attitudes: Attitudes are difficult to determine because of her façade of competent fluency however she is able to express or rather show evidence of a depression...

Self awareness, insight: Of her self-awareness would seem to be very much impaired at the present time although she is seemingly making conscious and strenuous efforts to gain insight, but there is too great a facility in her manner and attitudes for this to appear and progress at the present time.

Attitudes toward the future: With regard to the future she is at the moment not making any spontaneous admission of any ambition…

FORMULATION:

It is felt therefore, and in summary that this patient has sustained deprivation in all spheres, oral, anal and oedipal and throughout her life until college years…It is felt that a large area of her control are of a super ego character…

PRESCRIPTION:

Continued hospitalization is proposed for this patient at the present time and psychotherapy which is felt that she will require for some considerable time possibly up to four or five years.

Robert Ball, M.D.

[From McLean Hospital Records]

Seidner, Miss Marian; Age: 24; 3/30/59 and 4/2/59

Psychological Report: Rorschach, TAT, SCT, DAP

Test Behavior: Miss Seidner was friendly and pleasant but confined her remarks almost entirely to the testing situation…on both the Rorschach and the TAT she gave an unusually large number of responses…so unusually perceived that it was often impossible to determine the quality or nature of these responses.

In summary…there is evidence for a very active and vivid fantasy life which is utilizing much of her energy, allowing little for productive expression of her high abilities…she tends to intellectualize to a great extent, isolates feelings from ideas, is given to obsessional rumination and uses reaction formation and undoing…would strongly suggest that she is a suicide risk.

Although none of her perceptions are actually bizarre or psychotic in character, she sees the world in such an unusual, idiosyncratic way and sees so little of the more conventional concepts and is so overwhelmed by her own fantasies, that she must be seen as highly vulnerable to the possibility of a more psychotic solution…the rigidity of her defensive structure would make her quite difficult to reach and to work with in psychotherapy.

Irene R. Pierce, PhD

Psychologist

GOOD NEWS: I NOW have ground privileges: I can come and go without being leashed to a watchdog!

Beautiful day, brisk but not cold, I'm just in my green sweater. Hair tied back, looking good—not puking and getting some sleep makes a difference—guess this is what being healthy feels like.

How come that old weirdo has ground privileges, when I haven't? He looks mad as a hatter, bent over, '20s-type tennis outfit, grinning and blabbing to himself… And there's that skinny old lady in the long dress and loony hat, straight out of Great Expectations—Miss Havisham—except this one outdoes the original.

Heading for the art studio, might as well create, create, create. Lars is intriguing; what's he doing here, where's he from? Interesting face, penetrating gaze. At the least, not nuts.

Uh-oh. Here come the scary duo, the fierce woman and her dog. She looks just like a crazy ex-movie queen, angry eyes, lipstick overboard, short hair, nasty outfit: mean suit and ugly shoes. Dog even worse. How come these two are on the loose? Stay out of their way. Don't even look in her direction and rattle her cage.

The studio is down a flight of stairs.

"Hi. So you're alone today."

"Hi, Lars. Yeah, they unleashed me. I guess I'm not as crazy as I look."

Let him know you're not as dumb as you look either.

Create, create, create.

"What's up with that crazy woman and dog? How come she has a dog, and how come they're on the loose? They scared the hell out of me coming over here."

He chuckles.

"Oh, that's Joanie Hanscom. She's sure the dirty Commies are out to get her. No need to worry, unless you're dressed in red—she can't stand the dirty-Commie-color red. But I wouldn't worry about Joanie. She's been here forever, and hasn't killed a dirty Commie yet."

"But how about the dog?"

"The dog's supposedly therapeutic. They march around together, scaring the natives. Don't let them worry you."

Putting some clay back in a container, "And now that you've made it, what would you like to do?"

Create, create, create.

"Got a big pad of paper and some charcoal around here?"

"Sure, we have it all—we have oils and pastels, if you want."

"Color is too much trouble. I like black and white; keep it simple."

Soft black charcoal is fabulous. Portraits just appear, no need to think. Eyes out of the darkness…always eyes out of the darkness. This is easy, this is fast, this is interesting, this is the way to go.

He's looking; he's impressed.

"I'm a sculptor. Have you ever tried clay? You'd be good at it."

"Too much trouble."

He smiles. "See you tomorrow?"

Bull's-eye!

❋ ❋ ❋

JOURNAL ENTRY: MARCH 25, Wednesday —

There is still a curious fascination in being brought together with a widely diversified group of aberrations, in a *tabula rasa* kind of environment—it all makes for a new kind of biblical/Freudian perspective. I sort of have the feeling that I'm reading an intricate detective story and haven't any idea of how the strings will tie together—the only trouble is, I'm in the story, and I'm not convinced the ending will be neat or simple; in fact, I'm not convinced, at this point, that there will be an ending.

[From McLean Hospital Records]

April 6. 1959

"This patient appears better in herself but is rather restive. She is requesting many more privileges but is not as yet allowed off the grounds unless accompanied. She appears occupied most of the day and active but although appearing to be within a group of patients she is not apparently making any close contacts and it is noted by the staff that she tends to mingle with those patients who are more integrated. Psychological test has been requested and the patient is being transferred to WBI."

Robert E. Ball, M.D./cmg

JOURNAL ENTRY—

At last! I'm being transferred to an open ward! Belknap! This is going to be more like it—no more locked doors—it's spring, and everything's opening up—doors, buds, who knows what else!

I haven't binged and puked once since I got here—it's scary—maybe I don't even belong.

It's a great day for a new beginning. It's April, and I'm wearing my red turtleneck, no need for a sweater. Suitcase in hand, heading for my upgrade to, sigh, an open ward. No need for the jangle of keys, I'm in and out at will. Out into the sunshine or to the studio, back to the dorm, whoops, nuthouse, without ringing for a jail keeper. This will be more like it!

Belknap looks like a Smith dorm, not as big as Morrow House. The front door opens easily, and I'm in the entry. Living area to the left, hall to the right.

Oh my god! What's she doing here—the weirdo with the dog—Joanie Hanscom—focused on me and muttering, coming down the hall!

"Dirty Commie!"

Shit. I'm wearing red.

I can't believe this, it can't be happening. I'm in a nuthouse confronting the craziest duo in creation, both growling at me. How could this be happening?

I'm staring back.

This is unreal. Totally unreal. Unreal, but, in reality, pretty funny.

It may be funny, but don't laugh...

Don't laugh. Don't laugh. Don't laugh.

I can't help it. I laugh right in her face, and that of her dog. They both look at me.

Uh-oh.

Joanie's face relaxes. A big smile, then a chuckle, then a weird high-pitched laugh.

"Need any help?" A nurse shows up, and all three take me to my room.

I like my new room—same bed and bureau as before, but bigger and sunnier—the windows don't have bars. I guess Joanie and her dog are my new friends—they're sitting here, smiling, watching me unpack. Joanie whips a flute out of her suit jacket pocket and starts to play. It's plaintive, but it's nice.

"You're good. I like that tune."

She plays her flute while I unpack and the dog watches us both.

※ ※ ※

JOURNAL ENTRY: APRIL 12, Sunday —

The good news is it's easy to make friends here. They may have problems, but they're not problems themselves. There's Laura Weaver, a long limbed blond, who looks like she stepped out of a medieval painting. Laura and I are getting to be friends. Her story? Her psychiatrist husband had her committed. He tired of her after she put him through med school. Unbelievable? Yes. Do I believe it? Yes.

Sheila Burlie, an attractive young woman, doesn't talk much. She had been living in London, happily married to a British diplomat. One day he told her he didn't love her and left.

Hannah Ford, Amy Kallman, what are they doing here? Hannah's never around, and Amy spends most evenings watching TV, with her shampooed hair wrapped in a towel, eyes glazed, nails manicured. What's her problem?

Someone said if you put everyone's problems in a pile, and asked them to choose, they'd choose the one they understand the best: their own. I wouldn't. My problem is a secret that nobody understands. I'd rather be an alcoholic.

Joanie Hanscom follows me around, reciting Emily Dickinson, playing her flute, complaining about the latest dirty Commie plot. She's a great pianist, she plays the violin, she recites poetry:

> 'I'm nobody! Who are you?
> Are you nobody, too?
> Then there's a pair of us—don't tell!
> They'd banish us, you know.'

Joanie's not nobody—she's Joanie, a paranoid schizophrenic, who plays the piano, has a dog, and scares the hell out of everybody.

Me? I'm just hungry.

THE OPEN DINING ROOM, the kitchen, the coffee shop, the coffee shop. The Coffee Shop! Pretend the food you're buying is for your friends...sneak the bags into your room, close the door, hope Joanie and her dog don't come barging in. Binge, puke, binge, puke.

Doctor Meyer, Doctor Meyer, Doctor Meyer—where are we going? My nanny, my twin sister, my silent mother, my angry father—a good story, and I can wring it dry. The war, the blitz, the magician who went down with the ship—a heart rending account, hardly a dry eye in the house, but what of it? Where are we going? I'm hungry!

❄ ❄ ❄

PARENTS ARE THE ENEMY and their visits are discouraged, yet Mommy and Daddy arrange to see me. The shrinks put me under observation; I am expected to fall apart.

When they arrive we walk around, landing up in the coffee shop, where, I hope, we can keep a low profile. I'm sure they'll ruin my image, whatever it is. Oh my God, the guilt. Please, some one, make them happy. Tell them everything will be all right, they can drop me like a hot potato and it won't matter. Tell them I'm not their fault.

Back to Belknap from the coffee shop—I hope the crazies are on good behavior. Joanie Hanscom was on a tear this morning—stomping and swearing, beside herself, almost frothing at the mouth.

"What's up?" I asked her.

"The dirty commie bastards," scowling at me, "stole my violin!"

She was at her worst. Storming around, accusations flying, screeching out the door. She's probably still out, searching for the dirty Commie rats that have her violin.

Mommy and Daddy pretend they like my room. They brought me a gardenia plant, and sitting there with them, the scent is from a different world, a world of spring and senior proms. They talk away the silence: Katie this, Robert that, carefully editing out news of other people's fun and success, talking, talking. Finally—enormous relief—they get up to go.

We walk by the living room. Joanie is at the piano, dog sleeping nearby. She looks, thank God, calmed down. She's playing her own composition, a favorite of mine—the sound of elsewhere. She sees us and, *uh-oh,* immediately gets up and walks over, grinning.

"Mommy, Daddy, this is my friend, Joanie Hanscom."

Daddy's at his best, looking genuinely pleased.

"Oh, Miss Hanscom, Marian's told us of your many talents. Of course the piano, and the violin. I'm a violinist myself. Would you play it for us?"

Oh my God. She's bound to go off like a time bomb. I steel myself.

Joanie's crazy grin fades and her expression changes to unspeakable rage, wildly lipsticked lips turned down, clenched teeth, clenched fists. Then she looks at Daddy, standing and smiling at her, all old world courtesy. The lips and eyes relax. I can't believe it; she's smiling back.

"I can't play my violin. I lost it. I can't find it anywhere. Maybe when you come again."

She's back at the piano. I walk them to their car as her music fades into the distance.

A visit from my brother! Frank and I sit on the lawn watching an old guy roll the tennis courts. I love Frank; we sit together, not talking much. He's with the State Department, and he and Sue now live in DC. Looking a little sad—what's up with their marriage? He doesn't say, and I don't ask. No need for conversation, but Frank breaks the silence.

"A nice place, but you're not crazy."

I feel bad seeing him leave. He looks lonely.

A frequent visitor: Dan Kavanaugh, who'd stop by on his way back from Bedford Air Force Base. Dan and I, strolling on the path near

Belknap. A nice day in April. So tall, so perfect in his Air Force uniform, creating quite a stir.

He's so good looking and so smooth—what the hell is he doing here? I still can't figure him out. He's telling me about a big deal visit he's arranging at the Law School.

"Fidel Castro…He'll be speaking at Soldier's Field on the 25th. Do you think you'll be able to come?"

"Hey, Dan, what a coup! Good for you! How in hell did you manage that?"

"Well, it took connections. And pulling a lot of strings."

Fidel, the current big deal tour de force! How did Dan do it? I'm impressed. He's so sane; what does he see in me?

Nuts! They won't let me out for Fidel at Harvard. Dan's disappointed, and so am I!

I'm missing the evening party.

O fat woman whom nobody loves, why do you walk through the fields in gloves…Missing so much and so much…

SUNDAY MORNING, A CALL from Susan.

"You didn't miss much. I suppose it was a good speech, as far as they go —I didn't really listen. The guy has charisma."

"Right, right, but what about the party? Who was there?"

"I'm telling you, you didn't miss much. I mean the party was no biggie. Fidel was there, surrounded by his guerrillas—they all look alike in their uniforms—and, this was funny—"

"Was Dan there? Was he with anyone?"

"Yeah, he was there, but all involved, so we didn't really see him. I don't think he was with anyone– but you want to hear something funny?"

"Go ahead, sure."

"Fidel kept looking me over. Ben noticed it more than I did, and he thought it was a riot. He said Castro seemed really interested."

"Too bad I couldn't be there. Damn. It sounds like fun."

"Forget it, Mari! I'm telling you it was not much. The highlight was Castro's passion for me. Anyway, what's happening in the nut house?"

"It's not so bad now that I'm in Belknap. Hell, some of the crazies are becoming my best friends. Hey, Susan…"

"Yeah?"

"Nothing. Keep in touch."

❅ ❅ ❅

[From McLean Hospital Records]

5-13-59

Standing Orders: Miss Marian Seidner

Off-ground Freedoms (If permitted, describe: alone or accompanied, where, with whom, when, etc..):

"Out with family as desired."

❅ ❅ ❅

I'M "OUT WITH FAMILY as desired." A weekend cocktail party in Cambridge at Susan and Ben's.

A literary crowd, amiable, rational, good looking, boring. I'm talking to an editor from…somewhere…Little, Brown, I think…George Starbuck. Not bad looking, a little too edgy, but hey, he's not crazy, and he's interested. How do I know? Because, why else would he be telling me he's in the middle of a divorce? Uh-oh, now he's asking the inevitable:

"And what do you do?"

You really don't want to know.

"I'm in between things right now…"

He's hooked. I can always tell.

How did I do it? I guess I look more interesting than I am.

Time to cab back to the loony bin; George Starbuck should only know. Knowing him, he'd probably be intrigued.

94

Turns out I was right. Susan told him where I was, and, sure enough, he visited.

He's something of a catch, granted, but now that he's caught, what do I do with him? Sex behind the closed door of my Belknap room was totally creepy, why did I go along with it? He talks and I pretend to listen. What's he so interested in? I told him no more creepy sex behind closed doors, so what in blazes is it? Whatever it is, it won't last—he'll see through me soon enough. He's too intense; it must be the divorce. He won't last.

Walker Rowan visited, looking debonair, breezing in and out, surveying the situation with his usual wit.

"Marian, you're carrying your personal drama just a bit too far, don't you think? Couldn't you have settled for a nice hotel—a tad less costly—and much more convenient to visit?"

Walker's divorced wife was hospitalized with schizophrenia; clearly he's nervous about his batting average. He brought me a book about schizophrenia, Gregory Bateson's *The Double Bind*. I made the mistake of mentioning it to Doctor Meyer; the book was confiscated.

What the hell! Do they think I'm so fragile that if I read about schizophrenia I'll become psychotic? It's not contagious, for God's sake. I'm not a borderline lunatic, dummies, I'm hungry! Can anyone here do anything about that?

Goddamn you all, I'm heading for the coffee shop.

George Starbuck continues to visit, totally preoccupied with the book of poetry he's working on. He talks about Anne Sexton, another budding poet, and we discuss the possibility of a poetry reading in Belknap. Why not? It's easy to arrange.

JOURNAL ENTRY: MAY 15, Friday —

George and Anne Sexton left a little while ago; the reading worked out better than I expected.

They arrived at 4 PM, right on schedule. Anne is lovely: tall and lean, dark hair, pale skin, strange eyes. A kindred spirit—I'd never seen her before, but I recognized her.

George and Anne took the floor, with a bunch of us gathered around in the living room. He started, reading from his book:

'On Commonwealth, on Marlborough, the gull beaks of magnolia were straining upward like the flocks...'

My mind wandered, thinking of Marlborough Street, of what I was missing, feeling tragic and hoping I looked it.

Anne caught me by surprise, intoning, 'I have gone out, a possessed witch, haunting the black air, braver at night; dreaming evil...' I was right—a kindred spirit! I'm going to get her book!

To my surprise, my fellow crazies sat still and listened.

❋ ❋ ❋

AND THEN EVERYTHING CHANGED. I was in OT, working on my ashtray project, a blue enameled base with swirls of lemon yellow, a touch of white, a deeper blue. It all would melt together in the kiln, into, maybe, something interesting. An interesting ashtray.

"That's really cosmic," a voice from over my shoulder, and I looked up, at his blue eyes and wild grin.

Something clicked. No need for the quick comeback. I met his gaze and flashed a smile.

"Dan Hughes," he said. "And now that we're friends, how about a cup of coffee? Of course, I'll have to bring my keeper," smiling at his student nurse companion, "but it will be a party. And how do you travel—alone, or with security?"

That was the beginning. He told me he was Doctor Dan Hughes, a surgeon from the Peter Bent Brigham. We knew, of course, that's who he was before—not here. His wife, his kids, my life, our worlds—all yesterday's news. We were, like my ashtray, somewhere else, we were at McLean.

And we were off—first with his nurse, then without, it didn't matter. In the coffee shop, at the tennis courts, playing croquet, tennis, cards, it didn't matter, as long as we could be together. Laughing.

Guess what, Doctor Meyer, I'm not hungry anymore, and I know why, and what it takes. It takes me and him, not me and you. And it takes laughter. There's more than sadness in the world of the mentally ill, and we should know, because we're crazy. And we're together in a world that you're not part of, disapprove of, and expect me to give up. The hell I will. The hell with hunger. The hell with you.

After a lecture in the Ad Building we noticed a big memorial plaque hanging in the recreation room. We chose names: he was Joffre Guffray, I was Lenora Dockery. We lived in Florida in a big house by the sea and drank martinis on the beach at dusk.

❋ ❋ ❋

[From McLean Hospital Records]

Marian Seidner, July 6, 1959

There seems to be quite satisfactory progress in her therapy, both according to the patient herself, and Doctor Meyer. The patient had assumed more and more initiative as regards her privileges in the past month or so. However, at the same time, she had become increasingly involved with a male patient, Doctor Daniel Hughes. As was discussed with the patient, there were both constructive and destructive elements to this relationship and it was hoped that in working closely with the patient administratively she would be able to take a good deal of the responsibility of sorting out these various elements herself."

Signed, Phelps M. Robinson, M.D./cmg

❋ ❋ ❋

July 10

Dear Susan and Ben:

I type at a beat up old desk next to the cold damp open window. Your orange tree and a new begonia plant clash on the desk. Both look unhappy. George Starbuck came to see me last Sunday, bringing frankincense and myrrh and a begonia plant and the Sunday papers. I never read the papers, but I water the begonia faithfully every other day. George and I faced each other in the coffee shop, and then faced the wet green shrubbery on the gym porch. He will probably come again tomorrow, or the day after tomorrow. Today, come to think of it, is a Friday in July.

There's a terrible vacuum in this room even though the blast from my radio is making a good try. I have:

1. Played ping-pong with a schizophrenic who won't be convinced she isn't me.
2. Made ashtrays in OT with the patience of boredom.
3. Danced around the room.
4. Started and stopped reading Goldsmith's *The Vicar of Wakefield*.
5. Danced around the room some more.
6. Talked to Doctor Meyer
7. Talked to Doctor Haecox
8. Had dinner.

I am having a shipboard flirtation with Dan Hughes, which is more fun than a flirtation on a ship, because this journey is so very long. He is good company and together we hypnotized ourselves into a mirage: My name is Lenora Dockery; his is Joffre Guffray (we found those on a great board marked In Memoriam) –we have been married seven years (whoops—my name is Dockery-Guffray), we live by the sea in Florida in a big house with a terrace. We enjoy drinking martinis on the beach at dusk before the others arrive. The martinis are served by a nameless Filipino. The others are: a young couple whose surname I have forgotten—wholesome, interested, a little dull—but then so are we, and a middle-aged rake who has just returned from South America. We travel a good deal, mostly to South America, where it is too hot to sleep and the sand is whiter than in Florida.

Have you read any of Anne Sexton's poetry? If you can find a book of hers, I'd love to have it!

Love,

Mari

EVERY NOW AND THEN Dan managed, I never knew how, to smuggle in a bottle of vodka.

We had our private cocktail parties on the manicured lawn near the Ad Building, overlooking a myriad expanse of green. We toasted the day, the night, each other, and each and every nutcase walking by. Joanie, her dog, the lady in the hat and gown, all smiled and nodded as we waved to them. No need to hide our bounty—the others—doctors, nurses, worried visitors—all scurried by without a passing glance.

※ ※ ※

WHO PLANNED IT? MAYBE neither of us did—maybe, when you're living in a dream, there's no need to plan. Dinner and dancing in Boston—why not? Let's do it—a night out—a perfect night out—a night on the town.

I'm not hungry and I don't want to wake up. Let's go dancing.

It worked without a hitch. I had "off-ground privileges" with family; I signed out to be with Susan. Dan signed out under the 'supervision' of a colleague, Doctor Peter Crow. All three of us—Dan, Peter and I—drove in to Boston together. To the Copley Plaza, for dinner and dancing.

This is really happening, we're in a ballroom dancing, we're floating to the music. Tomorrow doesn't matter—we're in a ballroom, dancing. We're the best, we're the best dancers, the best looking, the best at what we do, the best at what we don't do. We don't do tomorrow; we do now.

The band leader is smiling, throwing me a flower—it arcs into Dan's out-stretched hand. He's smiling at the perfect couple.

Dan, leading me back. We better join Peter. He's looking a little piqued.

Peter's sitting at the table, watching. Dark hair, serious expression.

Is he angry with us?

"You look pretty beat, Peter, Rough day?"

"A terrible case in the ER. Young girl, suicide, stabbed and slashed herself... really meant business. Found by her sister. We don't think she'll make it..."

Whew, he's not angry with us. It's not us; it's some suicide he can't forget.

"God, how awful. Her poor sister."

"If she makes it, they'll probably send her to McLean."

We're back on the dance floor. We're part of the magic.

※ ※ ※

I'M BACK. PETER JUST dropped me off, and *eeek!* It's around two in the morning. There's no way I can sneak in, but—whatever happens—it was worth it.

I wonder if they looked for me?

Oh my God, they probably did.

[From McLean Hospital Records]

Nurse's Report

7-17-59, 11 PM –7 AM shift: Marian Seidner returned at 2 AM....seen by Doctor Robinson and given front lawn privileges only. To see Doctor Meyer.

JOURNAL ENTRY: JULY 17, Wednesday —

I'm nailed to the front lawn. I talked with Miss Mooney, who's on duty today, and agreed with her that there's no future in my relationship with Dan. What she doesn't understand: I don't have a future.

[From McLean Hospital Records]

Marian Seidner; July 1959

"...her contacts with him had to be curtailed in part. Transfer to Codman I was made, the patient needing the close supervision and administration of that type of hall..."

Signed, Phelps M. Robinson, M.D./cmg

THEY'RE LOCKING ME UP and throwing away the keys! I'm being moved to Codman!

Eeeeeek!

JOURNAL ENTRY: JULY 29, Tuesday —

Now that I'm on Codman, it's important to understand the rules of the game: Power sifts down from Doctor Stanton, to the chief shrinks at each house (currently, here, it's deMarneffe), to residents (Spalding), to head nurses (Poirier), to young student nurses and attendants. These powers determine your status: whether you need to be within arm's length of a bodyguard, and, most important, the number and extent of your 'privileges.'

Oddly enough, we all accept and adapt to these rules. They're part of our 'treatment plan', and questioning our 'treatment plan' is unthinkable. It is, after all, our last hope, our only ticket to salvation.

AUGUST 2, SUNDAY

Dear Susan:

Turns out Codman isn't as bad as I thought it would be. Sure, it's locked, but as far as friends go, it might be a step ahead of Belknap. Laura Weaver was also transferred here (what in blazes did she do to deserve it?) and there's Ellen Rangler, Maryanne Lockett and Barbara Raye. Not an out of touch loony in the bunch.

Laura probably freaked after her shrink-husband visited, and who can blame her? Ellen is a recovered hallucinatory, a Wellesley grad, a mother of two, and a worrier. Maryanne is beautiful and depressed, and Barbara's problem is a mystery.

Even the nutcases here have something to recommend them. Mrs. Carroll sometimes walks the hall stark naked, or curls up in a corner, but she's quiet, and keeps to herself. I love Mrs. Bradford, who floats around smiling—I love her because she is, in spite of everything, a true lady—elegant, poised, and very kind.

My room is great—it's big and airy, located down the hall from the nurses' station—it would be perfect, except it comes with my roommate, Carol the catatonic. Carol has dark hair, huge blue eyes that stare into space without blinking, white skin, and a rigid body. She lies there all day, flat on her back, no change of expression, movement, anything, playing the *same damn johnny mathis record over and over and over again*:

"Look at me, I'm as restless as a willow in a tree..."

If I ever hear that record again when—if—I ever get out of here I'll *scream*, and probably land right back where I started.

I'm seeing Doctor Meyer three times a week, the poor guy. I hope I'm getting somewhere, but how would I know? I'm still as hungry as ever—a bad sign—I think. He doesn't seem to care.

Gotta run—there's an organized trip to O.T.—can't miss the action. They'll probably hit the coffee shop afterwards. *Uh-oh.* I've been doing a little better, but there's too much food around. They have evening snacks—that's all I need.

Let me know when you can visit. I'll make sure my roommate's around so you can meet her (just kidding).

Mari

JOURNAL ENTRY: AUGUST 5, Wednesday —

If she makes it, they'll probably send her to McLean.

Peter Crow's ER case—the suicide attempt—she just arrived on Codman, in the room next to mine.

A former cheerleader at Newton High—now she can barely make it out of bed—what in hell happened?

Her name is Lily Michaels, and though she doesn't talk much, she listens, and we're going to be friends, I know it. I try to make her laugh.

How could she have done it? How bad can things be?

Another arrival on the scene: the eminent poet Robert Lowell, manic as the mad hatter. Wild expression, easily amused, lively chatter—he was actually doing handstands in front of the Ad Building. Hey why not—we're all children here—let's make the most of it.

Of course it's sad; don't remind me. Let's not think like Lily.

Best of all is Lowell's choice of female companionship: none other than my favorite schizophrenic, Ruthie Krauss! Always hand in hand, the Brahmin intellectual and the Jewish housewife from Swampscott, inspiring the following verse:

"Oh here's to Lowell in Bowditch House, where the Cabots speak only to Lowells, and the Lowells speak only to Krauss."

Why can't I speak to Dan? I'm hungry.

Last night a singer, Joan Baez, who performs at Club 47 on Mt. Auburn Street, brought her guitar and sang for us. She's a friend of Barbara Raye; she has a beautiful voice and her performance actually captivated our usually unruly group. Everyone listened quietly.

I ate too much for dinner and it's too early for our snack. I think Barbara has a bag of cookies in her room, but that's no help—I can't binge on her cookies. I'll have to wait.

Binge, purge. Where's my escape route? Where's Dan?

Okay, everybody, the joke's over: I need some *freedom!* I'm not violent, I'm not out of touch, and I'm not, all of your loopy evidence notwithstanding, suicidal. Call me a fake, call me a snob, call me an over or under-eater, call me a creepy secret vomiter, but, in the name of God or Freud or whatever you worship, give me a bloody break and a key to the outside!

More than anything else, I need to see Dan. I need South America and the house by the sea with martinis at dusk.

Binge, purge. Binge, purge. Binge, purge.

What am I doing here?

No, I don't want to see Doctor Meyer. I want to see someone with a key!

If I sign myself out, I'll be out, but where will I be?

Finally: Ground privileges! Thank you, Doctor Spalding, thank you, Mrs. Poirier, thank you, one and all. I'm on my way!

I'll meet Dan at the tennis court.

JOURNAL ENTRY: AUGUST 10, Monday —

Guess what!? Dan is doing what he always said he would: he's writing a musical show, and he's doing it for me! I'm the leading lady, Cassie. I told him I can't sing, but we both know I can put on an act, and that's all that counts! Sam Heilner is composing the music—it's wonderful! The play is about us—it takes place in a loony bin—it's a spoof of our life here. Dan even wrote a song about my recent tree-climbing venture—he witnessed it—I was up in a tree with the nurse below ordering me down—the song is called 'May I Climb a Tree?'

Anyway—Dan tested me by having me try the first chorus of the tree song—and to my surprise, I could belt it out like Ethel Merman (well, like Rex Harrison)! Mona Ouilette, who's going to be cast as Addie, 'the Belle of Belmont Hill,' really can sing. Jacques Goddard, a male-nurse-aspiring- actor, will be Andy, the leading man, and—it's so great—the cast will include a mixture of staff and patients.

This is so great—we're going on stage!

The music is beautiful. Sam Heilner is a real talent.

The show will be called "Close to Home."

[From McLean Hospital Records]

Seidner, Marian; August 27, 1959

At present she is actively engaged in rehearsing for the leading role in a musical on the grounds, and appears to be deriving considerable satisfaction from this. Because of the unpredictability which both her therapists and psychologist highlight she has been granted no further extension of privileges.

Signed, Robert T. Spalding, M.D./gmc

I'M NOT MARIAN, I'M not even Lenora, *I'm Cassie!* I dance, I sing, and I don't give a damn. Hungry? *Hell, no.*

I'm Cassie, and I'm so light, I float around the stage.

Jacques is a perfect leading man. He looks and sings like Howard Keel; he's a nervous Nellie nurse off-stage, but on-stage he's a star!

All the world's a stage.

Mona Ouillette, the "Belle of Belmont Hill"—off-stage she has panic attacks and needs a full-time nurse—on-stage she's a redhead who can belt it out like Gwen Vernon!

And all the men and women merely players.

Doctor Martin, Sten—transformed into singing shrinks, and—wonders will never cease—Lily Michaels has joined the chorus!

They have their exits and their entrances.

Laura, Barbara, Maryanne, all in the cast!

And one man in his time plays many parts,

Dan directing, Sam Heilner on the piano, we're all mixed up —nutcases, nurses, sickos and staff—it doesn't matter, we're on stage—we're not in McLean, we're in *Close To Home!*

His acts being seven ages.

Are you listening, Doctor Meyer?

"The plays the thing Wherein I'll catch the conscience of the king…"

Not "conscience," dummies, it's "super-ego" we're all after. "Conscience" is ancient history, please get it straight: "super-ego" is what we're chasing, what we're selling—it's the chief product at McLean, and it ain't cheap.

And yet, the play's the thing.

Close to Home, Close to Home, we're all in *Close to Home.* Rehearsing every day, singing our songs on our walks, in our cells, swinging to the music in our heads. I'm singing, Laura's singing, Ellen, Maryanne and Barbara are joining in, even Lily Michaels is waking to the rhythm.

We're all in it together, in Codman and in *Close to Home*—we're Ellen, Laura, Maryanne, Lily, Barbara, and Cassie—we're all close, and we're getting closer.

Lily's waking up, and we're becoming friends. Lily's singing, still shadowed by her "Special"—but hell, even bodyguards can learn the words. They're easy: "I am the Belle of Belmont Hill, Really appealing basically, Freely revealing much of me…" or "Can we tell what comes tomorrow? No, no, our time we must borrow…"

Ellen's troubles began at Wellesley, and when she asked for help, they didn't understand. Counseling? Never heard of it. Too weak for Wellesley, but just right for McLean. Her doctor husband and two little boys visit. She knits and worries, but she's our rock. We gather in her room.

Together.

Laura loves to dance. She stretches her long blond body to the right, then to the left, always to the music. She leaps across the room, laughing. Her shrink husband must be crazy. Laura is our inspiration.

Maryanne is lovely, with her huge sad eyes.

Lily *(how could she have done it)* is showing signs of life.

Barbara Raye. What's her problem? We don't care, because we're in it together.

We're all in *Close to Home.*

Close to Home: Dan Hughes's lyrics, Sam Heilner's music.

Dan's direction, Sam's piano, and our two shrinks' *tour de force,* "Diagnostic Tango."

> Both: We are brimming full of questions
> In our aggravating way
> With an enervating come-back
> To anything you say…
> We gesticulate with glasses
> Primly puff upon our pipes
> As we make our diagnosis
> Casting you into type.
> It began by suppression
> Went on to repression
> Causing regression
> To covert aggression
> And overt depression
> There's quite clearly displacement
> With ego replacement
> Simple denial
> That life is a trial
> And all remaining is id.
>
> 2nd Psych: Yes!
>
> Both: And all remaining is id.
>
> 1st Psych: There is symptom conversion
> A dash of perversion
> Some introjection
> And ample projection
> Back to the womb he has slid.
>
> 2nd Psych: Yes!
>
> Both: Back to the womb he has slid.
>
> 1st Psych: There is thought dereistic

And daydreams autistic
Oddball delusion
That life is illusion
He's slightly loose in the lid.

2nd Psych: Yes!
Both: He's slightly loose in the lid. *OLE!*

SATURDAY, AUGUST 29 —

Mona, please don't crack up until the show's over! You're our Addie, and we need you. Hang on—two more days 'til curtain time—we know you can do it!

SUNDAY, AUGUST 30 —

Whew…Mona's made it through the dress rehearsal like a trooper. Looks like we'll be okay! Mona, you're the best!

MONDAY, AUGUST 31: *SHOW TIME!*

Everyone's got stage fright except me. Jacques is popping sedatives, begging me not to miss when I take that flying leap into his arms. He makes me laugh. Being Cassie is a lark!

Waiting, waiting for my cue…it's taking too long…when I'm on, I'm great, I'm a star, I'm Cassie, I'm in love with Andy, and it doesn't matter if I miss a note—I don't care, and neither does anyone else.

Susan told me when she and Ben joined Dan Kavanaugh at the Casablanca and talked about the show, he said, "I didn't know Marian could sing."

Susan replied, "She can't. I'll prove it," and sang a few bars of Happy Birthday.

So what am I doing in a musical? Hey, when you're certifiable, anything goes.

Applause, applause, applause. It's better than they expected. Even the shrinks in the front rows were laughing and joining in.

TUESDAY, SEPTEMBER 1 —

Another show, another chance to shine!

Dan, Sam, Mona, Homer, Jacques and me—we're the greatest! Everyone's the best—we've put on the greatest show they've ever seen in a loony bin—and they're surprised because they think we're not as crazy as we really are.

I ask Doctor Meyer why he wasn't in the audience.

"Because," he says, "you're always acting out. This time you had a stage."

What the hell is "acting out"? If I'm always doing it, I should know.

The show was such a success we're doing reprieves!

Let's hear it for "acting out"!

✳ ✳ ✳

OKAY, WE'RE USED TO "room searches," which usually occur late at night, when some hapless attendant armed with a flashlight looks for such contraband as a hidden razor, Vodka, or God knows what else. There's probably been some security breach, and this is just another price to pay on our road to recovery.

Last night the posse was in my room, flashlights blazing, and, guess what! They hit pay dirt under my bed! Two table knives!

What? Who's the imbecile dumb enough to try and frame me with two dull table knives? Is it that wacko fat girl down the hall, jealous of my recent stardom?

Upshot: I'm restricted to the ward.

This can't be happening. I can't believe what Doctor Spalding said. He listened to my story, and then he said: "Miss Seidner, your Rorschach shows you're suicidal."

What in hell am I doing here? I'm scared, because I don't know where else to turn.

[From McLean Hospital Records]

Marian Seidner; September 6, 1959

"...two knives were found in the patient's room, hidden in obvious places. Although the patient vehemently denied any knowledge of this incident it was felt that the danger of not canceling her privileges was greater than the danger of canceling them, and consequently she is now confined to the ward. Subsequently she attempted to manipulate us by guilt and claiming that this was a major setback for her. Her need to feel victimized was interpreted to her without apparently therapeutic effect. Doctor Grunebaum will henceforth be her assistant administrator."

Signed, Robert T, Spalding, MD/.tt

❋ ❋ ❋

Do not go gentle into that good night...
Rage Rage against the dying of the light...

❋ ❋ ❋

"NURSE! LET ME TALK to a doctor with a brain. A brain that hasn't been brainwashed! Is there anyone like that around here?

I'm scared. If I'm not nuts, and I'm not, what am I doing here? They're driving me crazy. Where to turn? What to do? I'm starving and there's no food around.

[From McLean Hospital Records]

Marian Seidner; October 6, 1959

Marian Seidner has provided us with several really very difficult problems. The first of these was due to the fact that two knives were found under her bed. It has never yet been determined how these knives got to her room, and subsequently she brought some glass to the nurses, the source of which was also not apparent to us. She and her roommate both denied complicity in this and it was our feeling that they were quite honest about it. Subsequently she alluded to the fact that another patient on the ward might have been angry and vengeful of her. In any case with this as a partial reason, due to our inability to really grasp how this patient was doing, some of her privileges were withdrawn which became a major issue in her feeling that we were persecuting her...Later on this has come up in terms of real anger against the hospital and the feeling that she does not belong here.

The second set of things that have happened to Miss Seidner has been that during the last week she has taken to eating excessively and vomiting more and I feel is more depressed and looks worse than she did previously. I would believe that this is in part related to the knife episode...Her inappropriate laughter and our difficulties in really understanding how depressed this girl is continue."

Signed, Henry U. Grunebaum, M.D./gmc

DOCTOR MEYER THINKS I'M depressed. These guys are geniuses. Who in Hell wouldn't be depressed around here—locked up in a closed ward with a bunch of table knife wielding lunatics—fatsos out to get me because I'm not as fucked up as they are. Well, ladies and gentlemen, I'm getting there! A few more months and I'll be as fat and crazy as the next one.

AT LEAST I HAVE my friends.

Lily's beginning to open up. She was a popular goody goody, Miss Perfect who could do no wrong, a cheerleader, a class president. What happened? She's not saying. But she planned the suicide for days, weeks, until it was the right time. What made it the right time? I didn't ask.

I've seen her scars.

Her parents live close by in Newton, and they often visit. Good looking, vigorous father, morose and mopey mother. Lily tells me they get along, but sleep in separate rooms. Something going on between Lily and Daddy? *Shhhhhh.*

Oh my God, the problem's made to order for McLean, the perfect case! Freud, Freud, Freud, you had her figured out a hundred years ago.

We have the diagnosis, but—and here's the rub—where's the cure?

Silly question.

Guess what!? We're taking "Close to Home" on the road to Stockbridge, to Austen Riggs, another five star loony bin! I'm Cassie, and I'll get a chance to see Dan!

JOURNAL ENTRY: OCTOBER 19, Monday —

It was the best performance yet, and they loved us! Everyone was at their best—Mona absolutely shone—I've never seen her so relaxed—and Jacques—he's heading straight for Broadway!

A thousand curtain calls—Dan held my hand during the last—and then, to top it off, we had a cast party to end all cast parties. Nobody cared who was crazy and who wasn't—we were all in it together, and every last one of us, from Lily to Maryanne, landed up laughing. And I'm not kidding—really laughing—even Maryanne—I didn't know she could!

Dan and Sam got a huge round of applause from the rest of us, and a chorus of "for they are jolly good fellows, which nobody can deny"—nobody in Stockbridge, anyway—do we have to go back to the funny farm?

We do. I'm still locked up, with fatsos and fanatics, and I'm really beginning to feel like one of the tribe. Binge, vomit, gorge, purge—what the hell, that's what I'm here for, there's not much else to do.

❄ ❄ ❄

MOMMY AND DADDY ARE here for the weekend. I wish they wouldn't visit. The harder they try, the sadder they look. We go to The Window Shop for dinner. The waitress is some sort of refugee—tragic looking with a

German accent—Alida Valli in *The Third Man*—just what we need—the perfect extra in our drama.

Why do we feel so guilty? No matter what the doctors say, I'm not their fault. What can I do to make it up to them?

After dinner, a walk up Brattle Street.

It's fall, a scary time in Cambridge. The fun's over. It's October—just think what lies ahead.

Drinks at the Casablanca. I see Bill Cartwell at the bar, looking lonely. How come he gets off-ground privileges when I can't? That really stinks.

"Hey, Bill, come meet my parents. Bring your drink and join us."

Bill's a lousy choice for comedy relief. He's his usual brooding, depressed self. He's telling us his troubles—his need to "let it go and find himself"—he's "blocking with his shrink."

"Why," my mother interrupts, "can't you just be happy?"

Leaving the Casa-B, we decide to walk back to the Commander. It's a nice night, not too cold, and anyway, the drinks have warmed us up. All of us except for Mommy—I know something's on her mind. She's letting Daddy do all the talking, not like her.

Up Brattle, to Garden, to their hotel. I like the Commander; it's old school—not showy, small dining room with white tablecloths and old dowagers, no muzak—it's just right. In their room, Mommy breaks the news: Uncle Richard killed himself.

Am I supposed to cry? I guess I have a screw loose; I'm not that sad because I'm not surprised. Richard was like a runaway train heading for a crash.

"How did he do it? Who found him? Wynne?"

Uh-oh. I'm upsetting her. What's wrong with me? He's her older brother—she adores, whoops, adored, him…she's obviously feeling bad…I should just shut the hell up.

I picture Wynne, all dressed in black. What is she feeling?

Oh my god—the shrinks! I'm in for it now! My Rorschach and my mother's brother, both suicidal. I'm doomed.

[From McLean Hospital Medical Records]

Marian Seidner; November 6, 1959

This has been a difficult month for Miss Seidner. At the beginning of the month as the play was ending, she felt alternately cheerful when the play was reperformed and somewhat depressed as it was over. The situation was made difficult for her by virtue of the fact that there were several reprieves, the play being performed several times after what had appeared to be the last performance. At the time of the very last performance of the play which was going to be given down at Yale, the patient was quite depressed, and it was felt unadvisable to have her act in the play at that time. This was not merely related to the play itself, but also for reasons which will be related in the next paragraph.

Approximately three weeks ago, I was called by the patient's family who told me that her uncle with whom she had traveled in Europe and with whom she was quite close had committed suicide in England. They wondered how to tell the patient about this. I told them that I thought it would be best for them to tell her the truth about this, and that I would discuss it with Doctor de Marneffe. On discussion with Doctor de Marneffe, this plan was agreed upon and the patient's parents who were visiting the weekend were instructed to so tell the patient. This uncle is the mother's brother. There are several other people on the mother's side of the family who have committed suicide, including the mother's mother and the mother's aunt. The mother's youngest sibling made a suicide attempt which was unsuccessful.

The patient's therapist, Doctor Meyer, was also told about the suicide, and in his interview with the patient on Friday, he told her about it, feeling that it was better that he should inform her. The patient's family did, however, visit this weekend and discussed the matter with her, although they all found it difficult to discuss this emotional matter in meaningful terms together and there was some attempt to avoid it.

The patient continued then for the next two weeks fairly depressed and with a good deal of over eating and vomiting which has continued until the present time...

Signed, Henry Grunebaum, M .D./asc.

I'M THINKING COFFEE SHOP. I'm thinking sandwich, ice cream, wrapped up twinkie-dinkie, dried up tuna salad, chocolate milk. I'm thinking *lemme outta here*, but where is there to go?

I'm hungry.

They didn't take the show to Yale because of me. *Me!*

It's just as well. I can't be Cassie without my dream. Where is my dream?

Dan has been discharged. Back to his wife and little boys and home in the 'burbs. I don't even know where he lives. It doesn't matter.

His wife is beautiful. Dan told me when she drove him here she saw me sitting on a bench and said, "look at her: perfect for you."

So she's crazy too. Which of us is crazier? I am, hands down. She's not bingeing and puking her life away. She has a life.

"Will someone please take me to the studio? I've been waiting and waiting…how much longer will it be?"

Everything here takes so long.

JOURNAL ENTRY: NOVEMBER 10, Tuesday —

Something really scary happened this morning. A nurse was taking Mary and me to the ad building. Mary's always gotten to me; she's the sad young woman who just stares and never says anything. We were on the overpass leading to the building, when suddenly Mary turned to me, snarled 'you're the one', and tried to push me over the side of the bridge. My back was against the rail, and she was strong. I felt I was going over. That skinny young nurse, Joanne, somehow summoned the strength to pull us apart.

For God's sake, let me have ground privileges—don't keep me lassoed to these lunatics. I feel like signing my three day notice and getting the hell outta here.

[From McLean Hospital Records]

Marian Seidner; December 6, 1959

During the past several weeks, Miss Seidner has continued to progress in psychotherapy. She has continued to have episodes where she has been unable to control her eating and vomiting, but generally her course has been one of work in psychotherapy…We feel at the moment that she is doing well and we plan to give her somewhat increasing freedom to use and to test how appropriately she will use this.

Signed, Henry Grunebaum, M.D./asc.

THREE CHEERS, I FINALLY have ground privileges. Great.

Great? I'm happy because I can wander around the grounds of a nut house without a nurse?

❉ ❉ ❉

A VISIT FROM SUSAN. We're in the coffee shop.

"What are you learning with Doctor Meyer? You never tell me about it."

"I don't know. It's scary because I'm not sure. I talk and talk and he's pretty stone-faced. I guess I'm learning that Daddy's always been a control freak, pulling all the strings, treating us like little kids, and that Mommy's been too passive, always in the background. I'm supposed to break away, whatever that involves."

"Yeah, yeah, Mari, we all know that. He's a control freak, big deal. He's not that bad. Mommy's always trying. What else? How did they screw you up?"

"*What else?* Good God, I can't remember. We talk about some dreams I dig up. I feel like I'm not passing this course. I really don't know."

We sit and drink our coffee. Nobody interesting around.

"Something really weird, Susie. He's always trying to get me talking about sex. It weirds me out…especially once, he said I wanted his penis. *Yuck.* Another time he made some comment about my not wearing a bra, as if it was provocative. I honestly didn't think anyone could tell—I thought I could get away with it, not wearing one—I was really embarrassed. I know he's a good doctor, and one of the smarter shrinks, so I'm probably making too much of it."

"He said you wanted his *penis*? That is so *revolting*. I can't believe it!"

"Yeah, but what am I supposed to do? He's supposedly one of the best around."

"Yeah, well, he has a terrific reputation—still that makes me wonder."

She got up. "I've got to get back…What about that Doctor—Dan—the guy who wrote the show? Have you heard from him?"

"No, he's back home."

"Well, I've got to go. Call me. Next time I'll come with Ben, okay?"

"Sure, great. So long, Susie, thanks for coming."

SPEAKING OF SEX, HOW come everybody's name is Dan?

Wow, are they on opposite ends of the spectrum: Sane Dan and Crazy Dan.

I can understand Crazy, but why hasn't Sane given up on me? He still visits.

They all visit, but it's just a lark for Walker and George, visiting a nut house; it's good material for their next dramatic work.

Sane Dan is beginning to grow on me.

[From McLean Hospital Medical Records]

Marian Seidner; December 6, 1959

…occasionally mocking of the nurses, whom she feels probably justifiably intellectually superior to…

❀ ❀ ❀

WHY DO I HAVE to open *my big mouth?*

Here's what happened:

I love Mrs. Bradford, floating around the ward like elegant good tidings, always dignified, always polite, always crazy, but so what, always a perfect example of a bygone era.

Everyone respects her and calls her "Mrs. Bradford," except, that is, for that bitch charge nurse, Ann Hall. "Miss Hall" has it in for Mrs. Bradford, God only knows why. (And they think we're crazy!) Damn. "Miss Hall" insists on calling Mrs. Bradford by her first name, Priscilla.

This morning I was behind Mrs. Bradford at the nurses' station.

"What is it, Priscilla?"

"Her name, to you, is Mrs. Bradford."

That did it. The bitch took away all my privileges. I'm back where I started.

❋ ❋ ❋

"...She has formed relationships with several of the other female patients on the ward and seems to enjoy these relationships..."

Friends: Lily Michaels, Laura Weaver, Ellen Rangler, Maryanne Lockett, Barbara Ray.

If it wasn't for my friends I'd—whoops, I almost said it: "slit my wrists." Correction: If it wasn't for my friends, I'd be in trouble.

Lily, Lily, don't worry so much. No one's going to send you to Met State. You're attractive, you're sane, you're going to get the hell out of here and go back where you came from in one piece. You are not going to pieces, so forget about Met State. Come on, Lily, when we get out, we're going to have fun together: the beach, parties, lots of men. Forget about Met State, keep thinking *out*.

Laura, what's happening? You're not suicidal, why are you on Special? Why are they watching you, guarding you, what did you do? What the hell is going on, and why didn't you tell us?

Ellen, you're so lucky, and you don't even know it. Your nice husband, your two little boys, your knitting, your future. The voices are gone and they're not coming back; you're fine—you're the best. Get the hell out of here and go back home where you belong.

Maryanne, Maryanne. None of us know why you look so sad. Why don't you talk to us?

Hey, Barbara, I don't get it. You're upbeat, you're rational, you have a family and friends—what the hell are you doing here? Are you secretly nuts, like me?

[From McLean Hospital Medical Records]

Marian Seidner; January, 1960

During the past month, Miss Seidner has continued to progress nicely. She has been permitted to have increasing activities and privileges to arrange at her own convenience, going out evenings on a couple of dates with Mr. Kavanaugh, seeing her family, going out with another patient, Miss Michaels, to the movies, and shopping with nurses. During all of this, she has conducted herself in a fashion we felt to be quite appropriate.

THANK GOD, THEY'RE FINALLY loosening the reins. Apparently I'm "doing better," or "showing improvement," or a "therapeutic triumph" (just threw that in for a laugh), because, eureka, I have off-ground privileges. Irony: I'm no less nutty than the day I walked in here.

Shhhhhhh.

The only problem: I lost my dream (where's Joffre Guffray?) and I can't find my future.

GREAT NEWS: LAURA ESCAPED!

Everyone's in a tizzy; they were guarding her like Fort Knox. How did she do it?

Good going, Laura! You always were our inspiration!

Lily, Ellen, Maryanne, Barbara: how about a jail break?

Not a chance, I know.

I've got to find a future, then I'm outta here.

Meanwhile, we're taking it one step at a time: a movie here, a beach trip there, they're even letting me out to party with "Mr. Kavanaugh."

New man in my life, (if you can call this a life): John Donat, a youngish patient. His chief attributes: he's in touch with reality, he's good looking, and he has a sense of humor. Other than that, there's not much to say, but around here, nothing else matters. He has off-ground privileges, so we're going to Harvard Square together tonight. Club 47, here we come!

JOURNAL ENTRY: MARCH 12, Saturday—

Last night was fun. John and I took a bus in to Cambridge from Waverley Square. John pointed to an ad in the bus that read "The mentally ill can come back," and announced, "Here we are."

Nobody cracked a smile, but we thought it hilarious.

In Harvard Square, John asked me to do him a favor. He said they knew him at the drugstore—so he couldn't—but would I please go in to Corbett's Drugs and buy some cough medicine with codeine. *No problem.*

Club 47 had a group, 'The Charles River Valley Boys,' not as good as Joan Baez, but not bad. John ordered two coffees, told me to empty my cup, and then filled it with the cough syrup. 'You'll see, it's better than alcohol.'

Damn, he was right. We drank the cough syrup, listened to the guys play, and the more we drank the better the music sounded—and we stayed perfectly lucid—the codeine was great. As we were leaving, Keith Highet, Susie and Ben's friend, was coming in.

"Hi, Marian, *blah, blah,* where are you living now?"

"I'm at McLean."

"Oh. (Pause) Are you doing any writing?"

※ ※ ※

"Sing we for love and idleness, Naught else is worth the having. Though I have been in many a land, There is naught else in living"[1]

---

1   Ezra Pound.

I agree with Ezra, but look where we both landed up.

"In ranks outrageous and austere, the years march by in single file, and none has merited my fear, and none has quite escaped my smile."

By some smug poetess, whose name I forget, and who I wish I could agree with. (Excuse me: with whom I wish I could agree.) They've all merited my fear, and my smiles don't mean a damn.

"April is the cruelest month..."

No, it is not. T.S.—you don't know what you're talking about. What about September or October? January's a real bitch. Anyway, it's April in New England, it's April at McLean, the days are getting warmer, and it's time, I know it's time, to enter the fray.

Even Doctor Meyer must know that all we're doing here is singing for love and idleness. What's changed in the year I've been here? A ton of money has changed hands, the seasons have changed, my roommates have changed, nurses' shifts have changed, my dreams have changed, *but...ee-eek*. I haven't changed.

Laura knew what she was doing.

JOURNAL ENTRY: APRIL 29, Friday —

As Wynne always used to say, 'He who pays the piper calls the tune.' Mommy and Daddy have requested a consultation. I'm seeing Doctor Zetzel in a couple of weeks.

[From McLean Hospital Records]

Request For Consultation: Marian Seidner
   Age: 25
   Sex: Female
   Date: May 12, 1960
   Hall: Codman I
   Requested by: deMarneffe
   Reason for Request: Evaluation of present treatment

MY APPOINTMENT WITH DOCTOR Zetzel is in the Ad Building. She sits behind a desk, and I sit across from her. This isn't therapy; this is the real world. I drop my McLean persona and pretend to be normal.

"What would you do if your parents couldn't afford McLean?"

"I guess I'd get a job."

That does it. They're moving me to Appleton, an open ward, and I'm on my way.

How would Lily have answered? "I'd land up at Met State?"

Poor Lily—we've got to get her out of here.

What would Ellen have said? "I'd go home to my husband?"

Maryanne? A mystery. Mysteries stay here for years.

Barbara? What's she doing here, anyway? What would she have said? Laura did the right thing! She got away.

Whatever happens, we're all friends forever.

[From McLean Hospital Records]

Findings:

   Although she still tends to a somewhat nihilistic, self defeatist position, I do not believe she is seriously disturbed as her history progress suggest. She is neither psychotic or a genuine suicidal risk at present—and I feel mobilization towards discharge to be strongly indicated.

   June 1, 1960
   Elizabeth Zetzel
   Signature of Consultant

I'M ON MY WAY. Not really. I'm halfway on my way. Half in, half out. Out days, in nights.

The first stop is Doctor Meyer's office, at Shrink's Row, on Beacon Street in Brookline. A few blocks from Coolidge Corner, with its S.S. Pierce building, its kosher deli's, its hotsy-totsy clothing stores, and its tempting restaurants. Right on the Green Line, a real convenience, unless you've binged the time away and need to catch a cab.

Why am I seeing Doctor Meyer?

Where else is there to turn?

I've graduated from therapy to analysis. Five times a week, flat on my back, on the couch. Him behind me, thinking God only knows what. And guess what I'm thinking? I'm thinking: S.O.S.

He doesn't talk much, and sometimes I don't either. What the hell is there to say? He doesn't want to hear what's really on my mind: *food*. He thinks I'm blocking when I tell him what I'm most afraid of: *fat*.

Okay, okay, I'm so afraid to face whatever made me crazy that I cover my tracks by eating and puking. But Doctor Meyer, don't you understand? I'm not afraid of my past, I'm afraid of my future. I can't find it.

I check in at 26D Shepard Street. Nancy and Linda are engaged, and out of the picture, but the new roommates hardly make a difference. There's Connie Miller, Sally St. John and Nancy Veeder. Connie, a square jawed serious student, is at the School of Design, Nancy, very likeable with her cute face and loud laugh, is a social worker, and Sally, attractive but pompous, is a graduate student in international affairs. It's the same old stage set with different players.

Sally will be moving on this summer; they've all accepted me as her replacement. Great timing.

It's a good thing Sally's moving out. Totally obnoxious, with her know-it-all expression and her put down laughter. We can't stand each other. Here's one example of why:

I arrived one afternoon when Sally, the great Russian scholar, was freaking out about our missing U-2 plane, which, according to US reports, was missing north of Turkey, with the pilot suffering from an oxygen problem. She was enraged by Khrushchev's countering that the aircraft was a "spy plane" shot down over the Soviet Union.

She was even more enraged when I remarked, "he probably was a spy."

Ha, ha, Sally, I was right. The Soviets arrested Gary Powers, recovered his surveillance camera, and even developed his photographs. She never forgave me. The bitch. What luck that she's the one moving out.

❋ ❋ ❋

June 24, 1960
Dear Susan:

Today is my official discharge date from the loony bin. I am no longer certifiable, so I have to behave myself. I forget what normal people do, but I can take cues from my roommates. Are Harvard graduate students normal? I'll probably get a part time job, one step in the right direction. Back to Simmons next year. Any other tips, pass them on.

I can't wait to see you in New York. Your apartment sounds great— First and 82nd Street — within walking distance of the Met, right?

How's the job at Thomas Crowell? Do you get together with Mommy and Daddy? Are they a pain? I'll try and call you this week, but you're never home. I guess I'm not either.

Mari

P.S. Re the eating? Of course it's still a problem. Was McLean a help? I made some great friends; I starred in a show. I lost a year, but I had no use for it, anyway.

OUT OF THE BIN

Back to 26D and summertime in Cambridge. Sailboats on the Charles, open windows, a slower pace strolling to the Square, and Harvard Summer School.

"Let's go to the Square and see what the Midwest is wearing this year," suggests Barbara Raye, referring to the summer students. Barbara Raye is out, no different than when she was in, except that now she has a car, and we have unrestricted destinations. We party with the Charles River Valley Boys, we listen to Bill Evans, we sunbathe at Crane's Beach, and we hear Ella Fitzgerald sing at Castle Hill.

The nights, of course, are different, but they're secret. The problem with the food is that it doesn't satisfy; I just hope that I can bring it up and get some sleep.

"Sleep, gentle sleep," the elegant Gracie Welles, sitting with her nurse, broke her silence to intone, "Sleep, gentle sleep, how have I frighted thee, That thou no more wilt weigh my eyelids down, And steep my senses in forgetfulness?"

Ron Strobel, a nice blond Harvard Law student friend of Connie's, thinks I'm smarter than I am and wants to get me a job working for Professor Freund. Paul Freund, the top gun at the Harvard Law School, the great constitutional scholar, needs part-time help editing a manuscript he's working on. (Excuse me: on which he's working.) Scary, but intriguing. I get the job.

This is perfect; Professor Freund doesn't need help with anything. I shuffle papers, read law cases, do some typing, but best of all, have the opportunity of sharing an office with this wonderful man. He and I get along perfectly; we both spend most of our time reading. I get a chance to observe how The Shining Light of the Law School will take the time to listen to everybody, whether an eminent lawyer or a hesitant student needing advice. Although the professor can certainly manage without me, I try hard to show up on schedule.

Oh no, last night, this morning, the worst. I can't make it to work. I'm thinking, call him and tell him you're sick. Make up a good story—you can do it. I can't. I think of the way his voice would sound answering the phone—I can't make up a story. I'm thinking, this is it, you're really crazy. Pick up the goddamn phone!

I don't make the call.

It's night and everyone's asleep. I creep down to the refrigerator. There's tons of bread and cereal I can replace before they notice anything's missing.

In the morning the phone rings. "Marian, it's for you."

"Marian, this is Professor Freund. I hope you're feeling better. Don't worry, take care of yourself, and come back to the office when you're ready."

NOVEMBER. THE NIXON-KENNEDY DEBATES.

I type a letter of congratulations to John Kennedy.

Law School of Harvard University
Cambridge 38, Mass.

November 15, 1960

Hon. John F. Kennedy
United States Senate
Washington, D. C.

Dear Senator Kennedy:

What really counts is that one who is elected
should also be one of the elect. That you are both,
and the second in even higher measure than the first,
is a source of great joy and confidence.

Your sense of the future as history will enable
you to cross the New Frontiers with courage and wisdom.

With every good wish,

Sincerely yours,

Paul A. Freund

Another year is escaping; where is it going? Doctor Meyer is taking it. I'm probing the past, I'm losing the present, and I still can't find my future. It's winter, it's spring , it's summer. It's the end of summer. A changing of the guard at 26D: Nancy Veeder leaves, and Sandy Speyer arrives, another School of Design grad student. I like Sandy. She's quiet, she listens, and she laughs in the right places. We're going to be friends.

Friends: Lily, Barbara, Sandy. Great news: I bumped into Ellen Rangler near Harvard Law, on Oxford Street. She's doing fine, she's back home, she's in therapy, and she might even get a job. What about Maryanne? Still at McLean. Damn! And why won't they let Lily out? Well, think of what she did…they can't take a chance. Anyway, Lily's got full off-ground privileges.

OH MY GOD, IT's September, and I'm back at Simmons, back to the same old Freud, *"Das Ich Und Das Es,"* same old lectures, same old exams. In one class we discuss suicide.

"How can you tell if someone is serious about suicide?" asks Mrs. Rabin. Several hands shoot up.

"Found by her sister. We don't think she'll make it."

The sound of everybody taking notes. Don't be crazy, concentrate on what they're teaching you and write it down. Behave yourself.

Lily, Lily, you can make it. Get the hell out of there.

They are letting Lily out more and more. We get together at her house in Newton, with its faux Louis-the-Something furniture, its hand painted wallpaper, and its huge refrigerators packed with too much food for anyone to miss. Lily's father owns a discount chain of some sort; the proceeds somehow land up in those refrigerators.

Lily knows my secret; she pays no attention when I gorge and puke in one of the upstairs fancy bathrooms. We go to sleep in her crazy rococo bedroom. Is she my best friend? Probably. All I can do for Lily is to try and make her laugh.

Lily, Lily, get the hell out of there. Don't let us all desert you.

Lily arranges a get together with her friend from Brookline, Kitty Dickson. She says I remind her of Kitty, who, for some reason, never fit into her neighborhood. Her Brookline neighborhood is upscale and Jewish; so is Kitty, but she's different.

That's my problem in a nutshell, Doctor Meyer: I never fit into my neighborhood.

Getting to Lesley College, where Kitty now teaches modern dance, is easy; it's on Everett Street, just across Mass. Ave. from Shepard. I immediately like Kitty; I like the way she laughs, I like her easy manner. The three of us have drinks and talk about the usual: ourselves, our men, what we are and aren't doing. Kitty is a divorced mother of a little boy, dating a great guy, Michael.

"Michael Dukakis," Lily says, is "on his way up, and, at the rate he's going, he'll probably be president one day."

"See," Lily says, on our way out, "I told you she was different. A nice Jewish girl, divorced, and dating a Greek guy."

❄ ❄ ❄

ONCE AGAIN THE DAYS are getting shorter, the walk down Shepard Street is colder, and, good grief, I'm tired. I'm used to being tired, but this is different, this is more than tired, this is dizzy, this is too fatigued to take a bus, and weirdest of all, this is wanting to puke without even over-eating. Free floating nausea. I tell Doctor Meyer.

Doctor Meyer explains: Nothing to worry about. Psychosomatic, a result of my conflict over going home for Christmas. Material for the couch. I should consider staying in Cambridge; going home will "set me back."

Conflict over going home for Christmas? Okay, okay, I've got to believe him. He's the best there is, isn't he? Mommy's a spineless wimp, Daddy's an out of control control freak, and I should stay away.

Conflict over going home for Christmas? The decorated tree, the chatter, the worried looks, the paintings on the wall, the carefully wrapped packages. I can't help it, I still love them. I flunk. I'm going home.

❄ ❄ ❄

IT'S CHRISTMAS EVE, THE night of the elaborate Seidner celebration; too many gifts, too many *vanilli kipferls,* too many anxious glances in my direction. I'm exhausted. Naturally I'm late wrapping my gifts; I even have to run out at the last minute to buy something for Uncle Robert. My mother momentarily forgets my fragile mental health, and says impatiently, "Marian, don't ruin this for everyone." Then the familiar look: *uh-oh!* Did I upset her?

The pain in my side is getting worse, and it's hard to walk without a limp.

Something is definitely wrong. Maybe Doctor Meyer was right; maybe it's in my head? Anyway, he's right about one thing: getting back to Cambridge. Hold on, don't let this "set me back," hold on and make it back to Cambridge. Just a few more days to go.

My stomach is distended, and it hurts to eat. Does that stop the binge-ing? *Ha, ha.*

This pain is unreal. Something is really wrong. This can't be in my head.

I can't move. *I can't move.* Daddy calls an ambulance.

Interesting Case

I'm in the Intensive Care Unit at Columbia Presbyterian Hospital, and I'm in agony. At first the doctors, after hearing my history, thought it most likely a false pregnancy.

What?

Then the results of my tests came in. Apparently my sedimentation rate, whatever that is, is off the charts, so they all did a U-turn and advised Mommy and Daddy that I might be dying. I have all the symptoms of some crazy terminal disease no one ever heard of.

I'll tell them what I have: I have *extreme pain*, so please, somebody, shoot me up with *something*, anything, anywhere, any time. And please, somebody, tell my parents something, anything, to ease their anxiety, and send them home. I can't stand to see them looking so sad.

Where's Susan?

❋ ❋ ❋

Journal Entry: January 8, Monday —

They've moved me from ICU to Harkness. Beautiful big room, window overlooking Hudson. It hurts too much to write.

Hey, nurse! Is it time for the painkiller yet?

❋ ❋ ❋

Columbia Presbyterian Hospital
Harkness Pavillion, January 11, 1962

Dear Susan:

I've been here for more than a week, and since the results of my tests are still confounding everyone, I retain my status as The Interesting Case at Harkness.

One thing all the doctors have agreed on: whatever it is, it's *not psychosomatic*, and it's not related to my craziness! *Ha, ha, Doctor Meyer!*

It is, once again, a beautiful morning—the Hudson is crazy with sunshine and barges—and turrets. Managed to find some wonderful Corelli on 'QXR—you can imagine the spirits of your sibling as she sits (upright) in bed enjoying coffee and view and Corelli with a big smile on her face *(see fig. 1.)*.

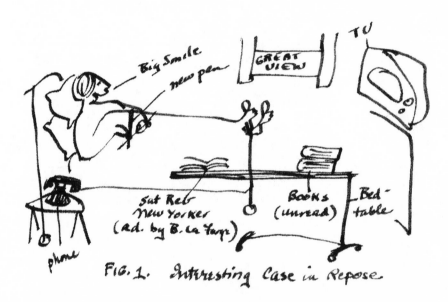

Big Smile
new pen
GREAT VIEW
TV
Sat Ref
New Yorker
(ad. by B. La Farge)
Books (unread)
Bed-table
phone

FIG. 1. *Interesting Case in Repose.*

Do you realize that my horoscope predicted I would have an unusual health problem in January? Honestly! I read it in Glamour Magazine last month. I thought better of telling doctors about it; am not sure they're up on astrology. A whole school of them came by last night and stared at me professionally, after which their chief, Doctor Somebody, said that whatever-it-is seems to be getting better. I asked if I could smoke. He said sure *(see fig. 2)*.

Moreover, he said, I could use wheelchair and eat solids.

To celebrate, I ordered nurse to bring me my sexiest lipstick and nightgown. And cigarettes.

Figure 2.
Most interesting case
upon being told she could
smoke. 4/18/62.

Did you ever drive a wheelchair? What an adventure! *(See fig. 3.)*

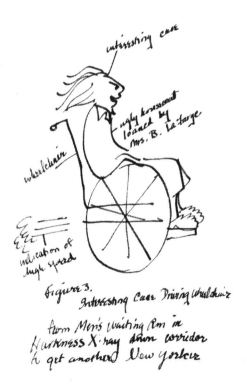

interesting case

ugly housecoat loaned by Mrs. B. LaFarge

wheelchair

indication of high speed

Figure 3.
Interesting Case Driving Wheelchair

from Men's Waiting Rm in
Harkness X-ray down corridor
to get another New Yorker

Call Mommy and Daddy and tell them I'm not dying. Bring cigarettes when you visit.

Mari

JOURNAL ENTRY: JANUARY 17, Wednesday —

Last night I had a relapse of sorts—couldn't get out of bed because of the pain. I was briefly overcome by self-pity—not for these weeks, but for all the weeks. This is turning into a damn diary. How pathetic.

Whenever I start to feel sorry for myself I think of the young Indian girl who lies in bed in the room next to mine—such sad eyes, and such weak hands. It's difficult to talk with her as she's usually too tired, but a few nights ago she had 'a good night' and we got to know each other a bit. She's been here since November. The pictures of her children look like her sisters and brothers. Such careful beautiful speech.

The flowers in her room are different from the usual arrangements; they're huge and wild and remind me of that deadly Hawthorne garden in 'Rappacini's Daughter'. I stupidly mentioned it and was glad she didn't know the story.

When Ron Steel visited he asked if I ever had the feeling that something that was happening couldn't possibly be happening to me. I guess that's what normal people feel like.

RELAPSE. THE JOKE'S OVER. If you can't figure out what this is, will you please *give me some goddamn painkiller!*

Weeks of doctors' rounds, doctors' questions ("Where did say you were born?" "Does it hurt here? Here? ...*Aha.*" "Is that in the Eastern Mediterranean?" "Where?" "Look up, down, into the light" "Can you turn over?" "This will cause a little discomfort...")

Susan told me Daddy asked them to give me antibiotics.

"Mr. Seidner," (patronizing sympathetic smile), "We need to find the cause. Antibiotics would simply mask the cause and *blah blah blah.*"

I'm feeling sorry for myself. I can't make it out of bed, so I ask Mommy to check on the lovely young Indian girl in the next room, the one with all the flowers in it.

She died.

❀ ❀ ❀

THANK GOD, THEY'RE *DOING* something. Exploratory surgery.

[From Columbia Presbyterian Medical Records]
Marian Seidner; Harkness 254; 2-19-62
Pre-Operative Diagnosis: Peritonitis. Cause undetermined.
Post-Operative Diagnoisis: Same.

❀ ❀ ❀

COLUMBIA PRESBYTERIAN HOSPITAL
Harkness Pavillion
March 2, Friday
Susan,

I'm in the solarium now, surrounded by windows and black sky, staring down the hospital corridor. Two people get off the elevator and disappear into a room on the left. Poor me, alone in a hospital solarium, staring down an empty corridor. Tragic, right?

Wrong. This is a picnic compared to being locked up in a loony bin. The service is excellent, with back massages at night, breakfast in bed, the *NY Times* delivered to my bedside early in the morning and, best of all, lots of visits from my friends. Ron Steel brought me blue and yellow daisies, which are coming back from the dead, like Christ. He reminded me of People Doing Things and Going Places, told me he'd take me to the ballet, and I had a moment of wanting to get out, have a drink overlooking the New York skyline, see a show, walk. Somewhere. But then I think of going back—back to the Fear, the Food, the Guilt, the Couch—and I settle back in bed. *(See figs. 4 & 5.)*

FIGURE 4.
REASON FOR WANTING
TO STAY IN.

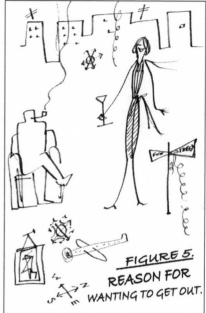

FIGURE 5.
REASON FOR
WANTING TO GET OUT.

I love it when you visit, and Jean Chace, and Ron Steel, and Dan Kavanaugh –he's in New York and surprised me—but, oh dear, Mommy's friends are starting to come by. Old Mrs. Stiassni was here yesterday; she brought some *Art News* magazines, and I thought she'd never leave. Mrs. Wallace dropped in and threatened to come back for a longer visit. They're so nice, but they remind me of how exhausted I am.

I guess Frank stayed with you when he was in New York. He was so funny when he visited—now that I'm off IV's and can eat, they keep bringing me custard—as soon as the nurse left, Frank ate the custard. Then he asked me to ring for more. The nurse was pleased: "Oh, you've got your appetite back." (She should only know.) Anyway, he polished off three or four of those custards, and since it still hurts to laugh, I thought I was going to die.

It's been *two months* but I'm finally on the mend. Doctor Aranow says my sedimentation rate, whatever that is, is way down. Mommy and Daddy still act like I'm terminal—how can I go home when I'm discharged? I'll drive them crazy by not behaving like an invalid.

Hey Susan, Doctor Aranow said it's okay to smoke, so bring cigarettes.
Mari

The worst thing about being sick

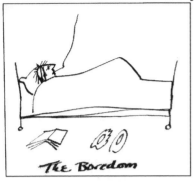

The Boredom

The Visitors

GREAT NEWS: THE MEDICAL brass says I can come and go as I please! I'm not ready for discharge, because they need to keep me "under observation," but *I can come and go as I please!*

"The only thing you can't do," Doctor Aranow loudly confided, "is take your boyfriends to bed here!"

I have revised my opinion of the medical profession. They really are well meaning and can even, on occasion, be pals.

Even better news: Ron Steel has invited me to a cocktail party for "theater people"—a perfect opportunity for my newly perfected pale pantomime. He's picking me up here, at the hospital—this is crazier than being in the nuthouse, and much more fun!

The best news: I look great. I've never been skinnier, so my eyes look enormous, my cheekbones stick out, I'm white as a ghost—sort of like the last act of *La Traviatta.* I'm going to wear my Sally Bowles outfit—the black backless—the total effect will be perfect: Sally in her swan scene, a Verdi-Isherwood production. I can't wait.

❋ ❋ ❋

HARKNESS 254

March 4, Sunday

Susan:

How come you weren't home when I called? Whoops, I forgot—you're weekending with Ben's mother at Mt. Carmel.

I'll tell you the details when you get back, but the party was terrific. I forgot what people talk about, other than their mental health and test results, so I was pretty quiet, but it didn't matter. Even Ron Steel—and you know what he's like—told me approvingly that I looked like Camille (is she the one dying of TB on stage?) and he seemed proud of me.

When one guy asked me what I did, I told him I was a full-time hospital patient. He chuckled politely, until I showed him my hospital ID wristband. He didn't quite know how to take it, and disappeared.

You'll be back before you get this but I had to write. And I need to talk to you!

CALL ME.

I'll probably be discharged this week, but where to go is a dilemma. Doctor Aranow agrees that Mommy and Daddy are overly anxious, and if I stay at home we'll drive each other crazy. He's suggesting a hotel until I'm well enough to go back to Cambridge; he promised to talk them into it.

One of the hotels near The Franconia would be perfect. They're old school, they're an easy subway ride to the hospital, and they're right across the park from you. I hope Mommy and Daddy agree. I would really drive them nuts by not staying put and convalescing, whatever that means.

I'm checking them out this afternoon.

Hey, Susie, don't tell anyone: I threw up dinner last night. I'm scared. I had to tell someone, so I'm telling you, but that's as far as it goes, okay?

I know I can do better once I'm out of here, so don't worry.

Mari

    ❊ ❊ ❊

DISCHARGE FROM COLUMBIA PRESBYTERIAN: Wednesday, March 7, 1962

    ❊ ❊ ❊

HOTEL OLCOTT
Room 617
27 W. 72nd St.
March 15, Thursday
Dear Frank,

It's only 8 AM, but because it is such a nice morning and because you surprised me with yesterday's nice leisurely phone call, and because it is your, I hope, happy birthday, I am writing you a news letter first thing on arising.

I was discharged last Wednesday and spent one day at home. Mommy and Daddy were unbelievably understanding and agreed to the hotel arrangement. The Olcott is the first one I looked at, and it's perfect: big red double bed, huge mirror across wall, modern hotel-type furniture, icebox and hot plate, maid service, unsurpassable telephone answering service, eureka, and an unbeatably convenient location. Right across the street from the Franconia. James Chace had aptly described the West Side as for the "emotionally unemployed," and I'm surprised how much I enjoy this area. It's solid *Burgherlich*, and yet across the park from my upper bohemian set friends.

Went to Harkness for a checkup yesterday, and my pals, Drs. Porter and Aranow, were satisfied by my physical progress. I am still a Medical Mystery and will have to continue getting tested and whatnot for a while. They are convinced there is no connection between my neurosis and the inflammation—none whatsoever.

I enjoy New York more than I ever did, and for the first time appreciate the joys of countless people and things to do. Cambridge is such an ingrown Academic Disneyland. I'm tired of egocentric scholars, ivory tower chatter, and the never-ending concern about landlords and theses.

If I do land up returning here to settle, my friend Laura Weaver, (the ex-McLean divorcee), would be fun to live with—only trouble with that is she has too much money. But there's no point in thinking ahead—I never do.

If I see a good birthday present I'll send it.

If you write: Hotel Olcott, Rm. 617, 27 W. 72nd St.

Happy Birthday, Frank, you are 30 now. Just imagine.

Love,
Mari

❊ ❊ ❊

I LOVE NEW YORK, especially at this time of year. The days are still cold, but not freezing, and it's fun walking up the street to the coffee shop for breakfast. I feel great; I'm skin and bones, as light as I've ever been, almost invisible.

"Lady," the fat guy behind the counter is addressing me, "you sure you don't want more than one bran muffin? You look like you could use it." I flash him a big smile, nod no, and we remain friends.

A dinner party at Ben and Susan's tonight. It's so great being skinny; I'll wear my paisley wool chemise. They said to bring a toothbrush and spend the night. Enjoy this while it lasts; the party's almost over, then it's, eek, back to the real world.

JOURNAL ENTRY: MARCH 19, Monday —

It's Monday morning at Susan and Ben's and I'm listening to Black Orpheus. It's been playing continuously and has become part of the day's rhythm; I hardly hear it. Music, come to think of it, marks different phases much more meaningfully than Freud. Forget anal, oral, oedipal, and think Richard Strauss during childhood, Gershwin at Barnard, Monteverdi at Morrow House, Theolonius Monk at 26D, Carmina Burana at McLean, Schubert at Harkness, and Black Orpheus in mid-town Manhattan. There are other strains, of course: Debussy, Corelli, Billie Holiday, Charles Trenet, Wagner, Mahler, and, oh my God, Bizet. The list is endless, but there is always music, and its memories are far more redolent than Proust's madeleines. And please, forget Freud.

Last night's dinner party was excellent, a perfect group. Hannah and Fred Mills, an elegant Armenian couple with unlikely names: Garrow and Griselda, Ron Steel, and of course, Susie and Ben. Perfect music: Schubert's Cello Quintet. Nobody knew anybody at the beginning, but by midnight we all loved each other. Susan's filet of sole Veronique was a roaring success. How does she do it?

How the hell does she do it?

God, I'm getting sick of that record but can't listen to any other, and silence won't do. Hate to feel this weak; damn, I'm supposed to be much better. Actually, it's peaceful lying on their living room couch, staring out the window after they've gone.

How do they all do it?

Staring at the sun through the slats of the Venetian blinds, facing the house opposite, smoking a cigarette. Later I'll go back to the hotel and be too tired to trot to a movie or listen to the radio or draw those damned faces—how else to murder time? Sleep, of course.

Sleep, gentle sleep, how have I frighted thee, That thou no more wilt weigh my eyelids down, And steep my senses in forgetfulness?

Before I know it, my future will be here. Back to Cambridge, back to Doctor Meyer. The party's over.

Why Doctor Meyer?

Where else is there to turn?

I'm hungry.

1713 Mass. Ave.

I'm back in Cambridge, and what would I do without Sandy Speyer? The 26D group has broken up, and Sandy has a little place further down the street where I can stay, until, that is, I find a place of my own.

Sandy's great—she's helping me look—and she's so Design School efficient, looking into closets and inspecting plumbing and whatever, while I check out the general layout.

She even enjoys doing it; what a team! Moreover, she has a brilliant nutcase brother, so she takes aberrant behavior right in stride. She's become my best friend.

Today we found the perfect place, I love it! 1713 Mass. Ave., not far from Shepard, close to the Law School, walking distance from the Square.

And, eek—across the street from the Midget Restaurant, a stone's throw from the Evergood Market and within reach of the A&P.

The apartment is a two room second floor walk-up, with big windows and lots of light. One of the windows, overlooking a little alley, has a ledge just big enough for sun bathing. Perfect! A beautiful blond is moving out; the landlady, Elena Kapelos, says the blond is getting married, and if I move out to get married she'll move in herself. *Ha, Ha.* Fat chance for either of us.

I move in. The two rooms are the same size; a stove and refrigerator in Room Number One suggests that Room Number Two should serve as the bedroom. I cleverly set off the kitchen area with a blockade of bookcases, topped with pots of philodendron, their stems twisted around string and attached to the ceiling. A patterned pillow on the window with the ledge, a couch and coffee table, and—*shazaam*—I have a sunny living room. This is home, and I'm ready for action.

Action?

Hell, I'm not going back to Simmons. Just the thought of it makes me want to puke.

Has anyone thought to check out Freud's feelings for his Mama, the beautiful Frau Freud? Has anyone analyzed the guy according to his own theories?

Actually, they undoubtedly have. Everybody's analyzing everybody these days, including Hamlet, for God's sake. Hamlet and Freud, both hung up on Mama. Both of them making too much of a big deal about it, but at least Hamlet tried to act, and left all the other loonies to their own devices. Freud had to go around projecting his own hang-ups onto the world and writing them up for us to memorize.

Is that what you've bought into, Doctor Meyer?

Uh-oh. Let's not think about it. Let's party.

SOME OF THE MEN in my life:

I met "Moose" Miller at a party. Moose is a former Olympic Discus Thrower, now involved in some sort of sporting goods venture. He is a very big guy. I don't remember the party, but I remember what Moose said by way of introduction: "Do you like the arrangement of the people across the room?" I studied the assemblage, and suggested he move the couple that was blocking the bar a bit to the left. No sooner said than done. He walked to the bar, picked up the astonished pair, and set them down as I had suggested.

Moose travels too much to be around much, but I look forward to his calls. Our relationship is made to order: sporadic, not serious, but a lot of fun.

Mike Duvall, a McLean alumnus, lives very close by on Shepard Street. Mike is the son of a British chauffeur, and grew up on the estate of his father's employer.

The family became so attached to Mike that they took over his care and education. They sent him to Groton; he landed up at McLean. Mike is tweedy and elegant, with an aristocratic demeanor and a sardonic smile. Underneath the pose, he's a hardworking student, a part-time athletic coach at the BBN elementary school, and a really nice guy.

He drops by frequently.

Dan Kavanaugh's civilized manner and dry sense of humor are an essential link to reality.

Dan Hughes, a.k.a. Joffre Guffray, still in my life, stopping by just long enough to bring back a hint of a South American sea breeze, the smell of a martini—then poof, he's gone. What's he running from and what's he running to?

And last but not least is Tim Hobbes, the most inappropriate match of the lot, but one of my favorites. I met Tim on the ledge of my living room window. Unreal, but absolutely true, just like the whole relationship. One evening I was sitting on the ledge, smoking a cigarette and staring at the building across the alley, when a voice right next to me said "Hi." The voice, right next to me, was actually to my left, and when I turned in that direction I made out his perfect profile.

How the hell did he land up on my ledge? I never even asked, and he never told me. With a Texas twang that matched his profile, he was telling me about himself, how he had to get away from Dad's cattle ranch, decided to go east, and landed up in the Harvard dorm across the alley. He often saw me sitting on the ledge and "figured I would join you." I would have been scared of anyone else.

Another dream, just what the doctor ordered.

He was talking about—I couldn't believe it was happening—horses and the wide open spaces. His age? He said he was eighteen.

OH MY GOD, JUST what I need: another dream. This is unreal, but he's not making it up. Joffre Guffray reincarnate as an eighteen-year-old homesick Texas cowboy.

Tim Hobbes, my new regular. We take long walks up Mass. Ave. when the sun is coming up, when Cambridge is deserted, when it's all a dream.

Doctor Meyer, are you listening? This is really crazy. An eighteen-year-old cowboy, for God's sake.

Doctor Meyer says no matter what I do, he's not sending me back to the funny farm.

But don't you understand—it's what I'm not doing that's the matter. What I'm doing hasn't changed.

Meeting Mr. Right

It's Saturday and Sandy and I are in the living room of her Shepard Street apartment. I'm staring at the Picasso print on the wall next to the couch, the black and white of Don Quixote on a horse, wondering if I like it. I like the music, Handel's *Water Music*, but the print is boring.

"Mari," Sandy says, "we have to meet some new men."

"Sure," I say. I tend to go along with Sandy, who generally knows what she is doing.

She just needs a little jazzing up: light brown hair pinned back in a bun, glasses, understated clothing. Lily and I have decided it's time for a new non-boring look for her: contact lenses, new hair cut, more make-up—a transformation done by two crazies. She'll love it.

"Tim," Sandy says, "is not a man."

"That is a fact," I answer cheerfully. I love listening to Sandy's records. Handel is perfect for my mood, kind of upbeat and peaceful all at once.

Tim's my eighteen-year-old Texas cowboy. Of course he's not a man; he's a dream.

"Let's throw a party. We can do it here. I'll invite some guys from work...Steve Diamond, Eliot Rothman...we can have Connie, Lily... maybe Barbara, Nancy, and some of your guys...let's make a list."

Sandy's at the Boston Redevelopment Authority, or BRA, loaded with men doing important things. This is beginning to sound like fun.

"Hey, Sandy! What about that guy you're always saying helps you out at the BRA—the one that gets the job done when you can't do it?"

"Oh, yeah! Frank Del Vecchio! Sure—good idea. We need to make a list."

"When can we have it? How about Friday, after work?"

"We'll need liquor. Where's a pencil?"

❋ ❋ ❋

SEPTEMBER 7. IT'S NOT really cold yet. Good, I can wear my rust colored corduroy jacket over a black turtleneck: a chic-arty combo, just right for my mood, which is relatively good.

Over to Shepard and down the street. Sandy buzzes me in. She left work early, but I see she hasn't knocked herself out, which is no surprise. There are plenty of bottles, and a couple of plates with bits of cheddar and crackers.

The doorbell rings, and here are Eliot Rothman and Nancy Veeder.

"Hi, hey, Nance, how's it going? *Ha ha! Tee hee!*"

It's party time.

I guess things are going well, the usual chatter. No thrilling new men, but hey, that's no surprise.

"Hi, Frank Del Vecchio."

Dark hair, medium height, big brown eyes, even bigger grin. What's he so happy about?

"I'm late—couldn't get out of the office."

Sandy left early. He probably stayed late to finish her stuff.

"Is there anything to eat around here?"

Whoops. The pathetic plates of cheese and crackers disappeared a long time ago. We probably should have gotten cold cuts or something. The poor guy's starving.

I look in Sandy's refrigerator: almost as bad as mine, almost empty. Eggs, bread, some bacon, boring stuff. *Aha!* An apple!

"Here. It's the best we can do around here. Sorry."

He's happily chomping away. What the hell is he so happy about?

Everybody leaves. They're probably starving. Frank insists on helping with the clean up.

He's probably interested in Sandy. She's lucky; he seems like a really good guy. And, according to her, he's brilliant. Harvard Law '62. If she doesn't go after him she's crazier than I am.

And speaking of starving, I'm going to stop at the all night Greek diner on my way home.

It was an okay party. About what I expected. People seemed to be getting along okay. Lily seemed fine; it's crazy that she's not even been discharged. What are they waiting for? Barbara Raye, with her loud laugh and wild good looks, is always in a party mood. What the hell is—was—wrong with her? She always fits right in.

"So long, Sandy. 'Bye, Frank. Thanks for helping."

The Greek diner or the Midget Restaurant? The diner's easier, the Midget's closer. But the owner is always at the Midget; he makes me nervous. He'll notice that I'm eating all alone. Again.

It's the diner.

Let's try and get it over with really fast

Nobody even asked me "what do you do?"

The bit about "I'm looking for a job" is wearing pretty thin.

❅ ❅ ❅

FRANK'S DATING SANDY, BUT for some reason we're often a threesome. He takes us both to dinner; Sandy doesn't seem to mind, and it's great for me. I like the guy—he's smart and funny—he really makes me laugh. What's wrong with Sandy? She doesn't seem to care; she'd be a jerk to let this one slip away.

Speaking of slipping away: Dan Kavanaugh's in Washington, DC. Moose has disappeared. The rest—Tim, Joffre, Mike Duvall—they don't count—they're too unreal.

Thank God for Frank and Sandy, some sane good company. And Frank really makes me laugh! His imitation of Syngman Rhee is unbelievable—he gets the accent just right, says the nuttiest things, rolls his big brown eyes—I hit the floor. And the wildest Gene Kelly routine—a song and dance straight out of *Singing in the Rain*—the tap dance is hilarious.

The guy is really funny!!

When Frank comes by to pick me up, he worries.

"You should really get your lock fixed, Marian. Don't you know the Boston Strangler's on the loose?"

"Yeah, yeah, Frank. Sure. I'll get to it."

"And that furniture you dumped in the hall. It's a fire hazard."

"It is? Wow. I'd better get someone to get it out of there."

Great Scott. Normal people make you crazy.

GUESS WHO APPEARS EARLY the next morning: Frank, with his younger brother Joe. Joe looks just like Frank, except he's tall and skinny.

Good thing I'm up and dressed. Tim's not around, and I'm behaving myself.

"We're here to fix the lock. And we'll take the furniture in the hall down to the basement."

"Hey, thanks! That's really nice of you. Want some coffee?"

They just want to get the job done and then they go.

This guy's unreal, but not like the others. Sandy's really lucky.

One night the four of us, Sandy and Frank, Tim and I, have tickets to a recital at Sanders. Sandy is really angry: Frank is sick and had to cancel. Sandy's angry because he's sick? What a bitch. I bet he's disappointed; I wonder how he's feeling. What a jerk Sandy can be.

She doesn't deserve him.

Hey, Doctor Meyer! What did I do to deserve you? I'm not going anywhere, and everyone else is, and I'm an island entire of self, shipwrecked, alone and... and, uh-oh, I'm feeling sorry for myself.

Poor me, boo-hoo. Get over it.

❊ ❊ ❊

A CALL FROM FRANK: "My Law School buddy, Arnie Zack, is throwing a party Saturday night. Sandy can't make it –do you want to go?"

Why can't Sandy make it?

"Sure. Sounds like fun."

"I'll pick you up around eight."

What the hell's the matter with Sandy? I bet she could make it if she wanted to—sometimes she's just too lazy to party. Lily and I have to work on her.

Frank's such a good guy, with his big smile and enthusiasms. She'd be a jerk to let him get away.

My living room is full of the sound of the blues—an old Progressive Jazz recording Ted Crowe gave me long ago –I love this number, Mama Yancey and her sorrow. Tim is leafing through some old *Time* magazines.

"Tim, that was Frank. Sandy can't make it to a party, so he asked me. This Saturday."

Tim doesn't care. He can evaporate, just like a dream.

It's SATURDAY AFTERNOON. TIM'S gone for the weekend, to see some old Texas girlfriend who lives in Manchester. A cute High School cheerleader, straight out of central casting.

How the hell did he land up in my lap?

I'm meeting Lily in Harvard Square—we're going shopping. Design Research has some great new things. We could even go to Chestnut Hill.

The phone rings. It's Lily's sister, Judy.

"Lily asked me to call you. She's having a really bad day and is staying in the hospital. She'll call you when she feels up to it…"

Damn, they're never going to let her go. Her family has too much money.

Lily, Lily, you've got to get the hell out of there. Don't let them scare you. You should have called me!

Damn.

I call Sandy.

"I'm sorry, Mari, I'm working on this project…"

'A bad day?' Lily, Maryanne, we all have bad days. Get away from there! Do whatever it takes, pretend to be normal, smile, dance a jig, come on, please!

It's been too long; they'll bleed you dry—you both deserve better and you can do it!

I'm hungry.

Shit.

Bread, cereal, jelly donuts, lots of milk.

Oh my God, it won't come up.

More milk. A full glass of bourbon should do the trick.

Thank God, it's coming up. Whew. I'm too tired to clean up.

The buzzer.

Oh my God, I forgot! It's eight o'clock. Frank's party!

He's at the door.

"You don't look too good."

"Actually, I'm feeling pretty sick. I'm sorry I don't think…"

"That's okay. Do you need anything? You look pretty awful."

He's all dressed up, ready for a party. Ready to go. What a nice guy, and I'm being a real bitch. Pull yourself together, just like you're asking Lily to do!

"I'm really not that bad. Give me a few minutes and I'll get my act together, okay?"

"Are you sure you're okay?"

"Yeah, yeah. I'm okay, really! Sit down, have a drink, I'll be ready in no time."

God, my eyes look awful, and the eyeliner doesn't help much. Hair's not bad. Eeeek! The bathroom smells. I'll clean up later. This dress isn't bad. Thank God my hair's okay—it's just my eyes, and my creepy expression. Cheer up, it's party time!

We go to Arnie Zack's party.

Frank tells me, years later, that's what clinched his plan to marry me: I pulled myself together.

That's as good a reason as any. Maybe better. He always knew what he was doing.

After that it's Frank and Marian.

Sandy's angry. I'm upset, to which Frank responds, "It's your choice. Sandy or me."

Why the hell is Sandy angry when she really never cared?

Tim evaporates. Joffre disappears.

Frank's plan included eliminating competition. He met with Barbara Raye to ask her advice. She said, "Go for it." Tim was easy to get rid of. He never told me what he did with Joffre.

He's different from the others. He's not wild, he has a brain but he's no intellectual, he's not in the middle of a divorce, underage, unavailable, or a self-centered snob. He's hardworking and takes care of things; he worries about my safety and, *ha,* my nutrition, and he insists on bringing me food, Italian leftovers from home, which I dispose of when he leaves.

Do I think I'm ever going to marry him?

Hell no.

He has a future; I don't. But we have fun together, and I don't want to give him up. Unlike everybody else I know, he's setting out to change the world. He might even make some inroads.

Consider why he went to Law School. He was a Navy pilot, when he returned on leave to see his family's old neighborhood, Boston's West End, being torn down. So what does this guy do when he gets good and angry? Unlike most people that I know, he does something positive. He decides the best way to get some power is to go to law school. He's admitted to Harvard Law with flying colors, and on his last deployment helps fund his education by playing poker aboard ship.

Frank is a guy who's never encountered a problem he doesn't think he can solve. Should I tell him mine?

Hell no.

We spend more and more time together. He moves in with me.

Doctor Meyer disapproves. It's getting in the way of transference or some damn thing Freud cooked up when no one was looking.

I say the hell with that. How come Meyer never disapproved of some of the loonies I was attached to? Hey, Doctor Meyer, I'm a sinking ship and I'm not giving up my life preserver, which, by the way, isn't you.

Frank takes me to Medford to meet his parents, whom he's really proud of. They live in a modest little two story white house with black shutters, set back on Marion Street. Frank's father, Frank, Senior, is—of all things—a balloon peddler. He's fat and jolly and a storyteller, full of ideas, always thinking and dreaming things up. His mother, Adeline, is a happy non-stop talker, good-natured, fat, sort of like an Italian Mother Earth.

Here's his Dad, a balloon peddler, and his Mom, with her spaghetti sauce, and Frank is proud of them and can't wait for me to meet them. And I'm ashamed of where I'm from? I'm crazy and he isn't.

Why can't I be like him?

Why can't everybody?

Balloons, balloons. Frank Senior has balloons in all colors, shapes and sizes. We take some home with us and get creative; we sculpt a balloon man, using egg shaped pink, long skinny black, more little pink, and, *voila*, he's looking pretty good. I paint two eyes, a nose, a moustache, and a mouth (I didn't go to the Art Students League for nothing), we inflate some more for him to hold, and then we're on our way.

Off to the Lars Anderson foot bridge in Harvard Square, proudly holding our creation. This balloon man is going on a cruise; I hate to see him go, but hey, that's life. He's looking fabulous holding his balloons, really lifelike in the fading light. Frank holds him up, then over he goes, floating, floating in the evening air, then landing in the Charles. The balloons catch the glitter (of what? The street lamps? The moon?) and we watch him slowly float away. Hanging over the edge of the Lars Anderson, staring at the water, no more balloons but lots of stars and laughter.

Frank's old orange Studebaker has no reverse gear, but that doesn't stop us. Parking is a little tricky; Frank gets out and pushes while I steer the car into position. He tries to park behind a fire hydrant, where there's smooth sailing ahead.

We plan to hit every bar in the Boston area, an ambitious enterprise that we undertake with dedication. Frank makes a list and draws a map, full of concentric circles. Return trips to the ones that have good music slow us down, but our progress is impressive.

We bring Lily with us to the Blessing of the Fleet in Gloucester, where Frank's dad sells balloons. Blue skies, music, the soft cadence of Portuguese, colorful hats, balloons and smiles. Lily, does this make you happy?

Summer is here again. Frank flies in the Navy Reserves and buzzes the beaches Lily and I go to—Swampscott, Marblehead, Manchester, Cranes, no matter the beach, there he is!

There he always is. We're always together, and I can't imagine life without him. But how can I get married, with my Major, Overwhelming, Unmentionable Problem? It's time to tell him. I'll scare him away, but I've held off too long—it's not being fair.

I tell him after dinner. Everything.

He's not as scared as I am—he's definitely sticking around! As far as he's concerned, my problem is No Big Deal! He actually thought it was something far worse, something unimaginable, possibly illegal. I can't believe it; he's relieved.

Maybe Frank is right; maybe I'm not as crazy as they all think I am.

I tell Doctor Meyer I'm in love. Doctor Meyer disapproves. He warns that my new relationship is doomed and will interfere with my analysis. It does. I leave Doctor Meyer and contemplate the prospect of marriage.

❋ ❋ ❋

MOMMY AND DADDY ARRIVE to spend the weekend, staying at the Commander. I've told them about Frank, but I know how they think; they probably think he's nuts. Why else would anyone hook up with me, their cross? We're at the hotel, it's afternoon, and I'm trying not to notice how they look at me, as anxiously as usual. I tell them a little about

Frank, how he was a Navy jet fighter pilot, sure to impress Daddy. It does, but probably makes him wonder even more about Frank's sanity.

Frank will be arriving after work, and we'll go to dinner. I wish to hell he'd hurry up. I love them but they drive me crazy.

Finally, Frank shows up. I can tell Mommy and Daddy can't believe that he's normal looking, even handsome. He flashes his huge smile, and I can see them warming up.

Then God intervenes and gives Frank a chance to prove his mettle: Daddy's car stalls—a major nightmare in his world. No problem! Frank opens the hood, fiddles with some stuff, and, presto, we're off to *Henri Quatre* Restaurant. That does it! Frank can do no wrong; he's handsome, he's a lawyer and an erstwhile Navy pilot, but most important, he has, unlike all my other exes, proven himself to be down to earth and capable!

We have a great dinner at *Henri Quatre.*

"There are more things in heaven and earth," Doctor Meyer, "than are dreamt of in your philosophy." Your Freudian suggestions fade into the distance.

Were those lost years? It doesn't matter, they're gone now.

We're getting married.

Eeeeeek!

Mommy and Daddy are almost as scared as I am. They're worried that poor Frank doesn't know what he's getting into; Daddy can't believe that Frank knows everything and still wants to tie the knot. He takes Frank aside just to make sure: "Do you know…are you aware that…do you realize…you're making a move you may regret…" Frank won't budge.

I'm scared because I'm still hungry. Maybe Daddy's right; Frank really doesn't know what he's getting into.

They go back to New York, and a few weeks later they call.

"Hilde Bruch, the world renowned specialist on eating disorders…she's interested and will take your case…a good idea before your marriage…it will mean living in New York…office on 81st Street…he can visit…you both should think it over."

Wow. They've scouted around and come up with the ultimate last chance, the All Time Olympic Champion On Eating Disorders, the International

Celebrity Solver Of Bingeing And Puking—an irresistible opportunity—how can I turn it down?

Frank is not impressed. We don't need Hilde Bruch; we just need to get married.

"But Frank," say I, "if she can't help me no one can. If I don't do this I'll regret it, I know I will, and you might too. You don't know what you're getting into…what do you think…*blah, blah, blah.*"

I'm going to New York. Mommy and Daddy have found an apartment on 90th Street, between Third and Park, a "cute first floor one-bedroom, convenient to Doctor Bruch's office." This might even be fun. Susan and Ben are in New York, and there are others—Ron Steel, Jean and James Chace, Hannah and Fred Mills, and Laura Weaver lives not far away.

I love Laura Weaver—she always was our inspiration—first she escaped, and now she's suing McLean Hospital! Three cheers, Laura, from the rest of us—Lily, Ellen, Barbara, Maryanne—we all salute you! I'll call you first thing when I'm in New York.

Laura's apartment is at Gramercy Park, full of antiques and oriental rugs, perfect Laura. She mixes a martini in her fancy martini shaker. The same laugh, the same medieval looks, pale and graceful as ever.

"Marian, I have the perfect job for you. My friend Mimi Rainer owns a clothing boutique at 83rd and Madison, 'BonJour,' and she's looking for part-time help. You'd be perfect. Let me call her."

"I've noticed the store—it has some great stuff in the window. Hey, Laura, thanks, it sounds like fun, in fact, I'd love it!"

Interview time. I put on a boutique-type outfit: white long sleeved dress, light blue and white chiffon scarf, elegance incarnate. She'll be impressed and hire me on the spot.

She does. Mimi is a slightly nervous, skinny, gray-haired lady in her fifties. It's a nice store, too expensive to attract losers. "Can you make it three afternoons a week?" Perfect. I haven't seen Doctor Bruch yet, but I know she's scheduled me in the morning.

"Sure. When do I start?"

So far so good. I miss Frank, but he's coming down this weekend. He'll love my little place!

My place is perfect. It's on a quiet street in one of those old brownstones, just a block away from Park, and two from all the stores on Madison. Plenty of fancy bars nearby and places to go—I can't wait for Frank!

I'm too excited to be crazy. I can go to restaurants and eat an almost normal meal. Hey, Doctor Bruch, I'm on my way—this might be easier than I thought!

Treatment Plan Number Four:
Doctor Bruch

Doctor Bruch's office is in a typical east eighties building. A doorman opens the door, and I take an elevator up to the tenth floor. She's sitting behind a big desk, smiling.

Doctor Meyer never smiled.

She looks a bit like Mommy: gray hair, well put together, friendly face.

"Yes, Marian, please sit down. Your parents told me about you, now I want to hear from you."

God, she sounds like Mommy too. Same accent. But she's worlds apart from home—she's the renowned Hilde Bruch. I know we'll get along—I can sense it right away—I can be myself, whatever that turns out to be.

I tell the whole story, the eating, the vomiting, the hunger, the men, the sex, more hunger, McLean, Doctor Meyer, and finally, Frank.

"Doctor Meyer never sent your records, which is most unusual. Do you have any idea why that would be?"

Because he's passionately in love and refuses to give me up? How the hell would I know why he does or doesn't do anything? He couldn't figure me out, and I sure don't have a clue about him.

"I really don't know. He wasn't thrilled to see me go. He was against my interrupting my analysis to get married."

"I see, yes. Well, we'll manage very well without. First, I want to make sure of your physical condition. You'll see a doctor, and most likely be getting vitamin injections."

A total turnaround from fanciful Freud. This is more like it. Hope at last.

Great, this weekend is Labor Day, a three-day weekend, and Frank will be here soon! Everything is great, walking up Madison Avenue is great, so is my apartment, Hilde Bruch, the weather—I'm finally Doing Something Right! I can't wait to tell Frank!

How come Meyer never sent my records? He was giving me the creeps, with his focus on sex and that disgusting comment that I wanted his penis. Thank God for Hilde Bruch, and thank you, parents, you really came through! I hope I can do my part. I hope I don't let everybody down…please, please, if there is a God, which there isn't, help me do my part!

❈ ❈ ❈

DAMN LABOR DAY TRAFFIC; *I can't wait to see him!*

He makes it through traffic and arrives on schedule, hooray, probably having outsmarted traffic with his wild jet pilot short cuts.

Everything changes when he's around—I'm not as scared—he makes me laugh and laugh.

It doesn't really matter where we go, but we're in New York, so let's do it right and have some fun. We try the fancy restaurant on Madison—too expensive for what you get—and the little Italian bistro on Third Avenue, much better. But it doesn't really matter.

Should we head to Greenwich Village? Why bother; there's so much happening right here. Forget theater—too much trouble.

(Who needs other people's drama, we have our own?)

We see Fellini's *8 ½*, the movie everyone's talking about, and it's pretty good—I love his music—though *La Dolce Vita* was—

Shut up, Marian, you're sounding like the worst of them: "How do you think Bergman's Virgin Spring compares to his The Seventh Seal? And have you read…

Give me People Doing Things…like Frank.

ELAINE'S, THE BAR THAT Susie said Frank Conroy likes, is just two blocks away, on Second, between 88th and 89th. I don't see why it's catching on so fast—what's the big deal? It's enough to just be walking down the street, going nowhere in particular, looking in store windows, stopping for a drink or coffee, it doesn't matter what we do.

Frank leaves mid-afternoon on Monday—he can't stay later due to the traffic.

It's really quiet here. I should go out, but where to go?

Uh-oh.

I'm really hungry.

There's a fancy bakery a few blocks away—bakeries are open on holidays, aren't they?

If it isn't, no problem, there are lots of other places. The deli is always open. What am I doing?

Frank, you don't know what you're getting into.

Of course I'll tell Bruch about my setback.

I know I can do better.

She is, thank goodness, easy to talk to, and unlike the Freudian boys, she *responds.*

We talk about what I eat and when, trying to pinpoint the triggers.

The problem is, and I hate to think it, it doesn't take a trigger, it's just me: hungry and crazy.

Shut up, Marian, and try, Try harder. Try to get on her wavelength instead of your own.

She's straightforward and she's even funny. She told me that one of her patients, skinny like me, was in a smorgasbord restaurant re-filling her plate over and over, when she was approached by a fatso.

"If you can do it, so can I," the fatty said, heaping up her own plate.

It's great to be able to talk and laugh about it. What a difference from Meyer!

I'm getting vitamin shots and she wants me to try and eat some liver—I must be anemic—I'll do whatever she tells me.

If she tells me to run around the block three times I'll do it, no questions asked.

❊ ❊ ❊

THE JOB AT BONJOUR is perfect; in fact, I wish it were more than three afternoons a week. Mimi is easy to be with, and very clear about what I'm to do, which isn't really much. I love helping her customers; many of them don't have a clue about what they want or what looks good on them, and they really appreciate an honest opinion.

And honesty is what they get. I don't care if they buy anything, and I suspect it shows—they come back again, and ask for my help. Susan dropped in when I had a customer, and we both told her what looked good and what didn't—she was so pleased she bought out the store. Actually, she was good-looking, and a lot of stuff looked great. Mimi was thrilled; she asked Susan to come by more often.

The empty afternoons are the toughest. Everyone I know is working; even Laura is going back to school, to be a nurse. Good for Laura!

Mommy and Daddy are writing to Lily's parents, urging them to get a consultation, advising them to really interfere. Good for them! I hope the Michaels follow through. Maybe they'll listen, because they know my story. Lily's been there too long—she has too much money.

These afternoons are really tough, with no one around and nothing to do.

Except you know what.

I've got everything going for me, I've got Bruch, I've got Frank, I've got friends and family and New York hot spots and cold spots and I'm sinking, sinking, letting everyone down. This is the end of the line, this is it, there's nowhere else to turn. Why can't I be normal, like the people in the street, in the stores, on the subway and buses—they have problems, but they don't fall apart. And I do. Fall apart.

Frank, you don't know what you're getting into—what you really should get out of. I'm eating and puking, eating and puking, and there's no end in sight.

Doctor Bruch is talking hospitalization.

See what I mean?

I'm a lost cause.

Bruch is talking about a place called the Psychiatric Institute, or "P.I.," a teaching hospital.

Big deal. Teaching-smeaching, what difference does it make? I'm hopeless.

The P.I. is part of Columbia Presbyterian, and get this: it's really hard to get in to.

You mean the crazier you are the better your chances? Oh boy, this place sounds great.

She says my chances are really good; she's on the staff, and they're interested in identical twins. I could probably get in.

Wow! Lucky me! Mommy and Daddy will be so proud—they'll tell all their friends.

Frank, you can do better. Here's your chance. Get out while the going is good.

What does Frank do? What he always does: he doesn't run away, but looks for a solution. He's logical and positive, a combination I'm unaccustomed to.

What the hell does he see in me? I honestly don't get it.

Frank says, "You trust Doctor Bruch. Let's take her advice, and give the hospital a try, but on one condition: no more than one year. If in one year you're no better, you leave the hospital to get married. We'll get married sooner or later, but no later than in one year."

We tell Doctor Bruch our decision and on October 2, 1963, I'm admitted to Psychiatric Institute.

Treatment Plan Number Five: Psychiatric Institute

If McLean was Ivy League, this place is Blackboard Jungle. Forget tennis courts, private rooms, manicured lawns, or eminent poets. P.I. is a stone building in uptown Manhattan, at 168th Street. Symbolically enough, my floor is below street level; one has to take the elevator down.

My floor: off a long corridor are two sleeping areas, a TV room, a dining room and a small nurses' station. Frills: a bench in the corridor, bureaus and cots in the sleeping areas, long tables and chairs in the dining room, a couch and some chairs in the TV room.

The men's ward is totally separate, on the other side of the floor. Something tells me there won't be any McLean-type mixers to get us together.

Ha Ha. Cut the sarcasm; it doesn't help.

There's no way of knowing what the weather is like, or pretty much anything else going on in the outside world.

Boo-hoo. As if you care about the outside world.

One thing you do know when you're here: you're in serious trouble, so pay attention and do your damndest to get out.

Get out? I've tried that and I flunked. I'm scared.

Shut up. Frank will be visiting this weekend. Get serious and stop feeling sorry for yourself.

Good news: Many of my fellow patients are young and rational, with invisible problems.

There's Taia, German, attractive, tough, who hangs out with Lucy, a cute teenager who eats dog biscuits and giggles. Linda is a skinny likeable sort, eager to please, Nina is fat, angry and articulate, glued to the TV, and Bonnie is a young blond with a nice disposition.

Of course there are the usual crazies. There are the hall pacers, hallucinating and hollering, there are the pathetic mutes, scared out of their wits, and there are a few nutty neurotics, like Mrs. Goldblatt. Mrs. Goldblatt's problem is plastic. I swear to God that's true. "I can't help it," she told me, opening her drawers to show me her dilemma. Everything she owns is separately bagged in plastic. My God, she's probably single-handedly put Saran Wrap over the top, and she can't stop herself.

What happens if they take away the plastic bags? And I think I have problems!

By far the worst, in everybody's books, is the huge smelly whale of a fatso who stinks to high heaven and is too obese to shove into a tub. She literally smells up the whole floor. The nurses tried forcing her to shower; it didn't seem to help. It's probably some sort of somatic disorder. She is so totally disgusting she almost takes my appetite away. *Ha.*

My admission procedure was conducted by Doctor Wharton, a nice guy with an aberrant (in his profession) unassuming manner. I told the usual story and took pretty much the same battery of tests.

Big mistake: I didn't play it smart and slant the TAT tests, etc., with positive thinking and joy. Damn! They'll be testing Susan, and since I told her how to play the game, it'll verify that I'm the crazy one. Oh well, that's probably true, so what the hell.

Our days on the ward aren't exactly thrilling or chock full of activities. For exercise, the elevator transports us to an upstairs gym, where we play volleyball. Taia is the volleyball star; no one else really gives a damn, except maybe Lucy, but she's too short to be of any help. Funny: one of the hall pacing crazies is a pretty good volleyball player. When she and Taia team up, it's no contest.

When we were going up in the elevator, one of our loonies, chock full of Thorazine, let out some weird side-effect tics with her right arm. Two shrinks were in the elevator; one of them looked at her, snickered, and made an aside to his pal. I heard the word "Thorazine" as they both chuckled. Ha Ha.

And they wonder why we get depressed.

❈ ❈ ❈

[From Psychiatric Institute Medical Records]
Marian Seidner
Date of admission: October 2,1963
Date of Summary: October 30,1963
Summary Of Mental Examination

There is a subtle thinking disorder. At present there are no delusions or hallucinations. Compulsive eating and vomiting, which have been a problem in the past, are no longer present. There is mild to moderate depression at present. There is no disturbance of consciousness or disorder of memory. General intelligence level is high

Recommendation For Treatment

To be treated with psychotherapy twice a week; also seen in occupational therapy. It is felt that perhaps her artistic talents and production will be helpful as an adjunct in therapy. Though striking initially is the patient's unclear view of herself, she has never clearly evolved any concept of herself as separate from her twin sister. Helping the patient to achieve some sense of self-awareness seems to be an important initial goal in treatment.

Prognosis: Good.

Doctor Ralph N. Wharton/hbc

❈ ❈ ❈

THEY'RE MAKING ME DRINK a nutritional formula, "Sustagen." So far I haven't put on any weight, but I haven't been eating much. How can I? This is a locked ward, and there's no coffee shop to go trotting off to. What a relief..

I need books. Good thing Frank will be here this weekend. The poor guy.

When Roberta Parnas arrives there is immediate mutual recognition. She's about my age, skinny, attractive, and relatively well dressed. An eating disorder! Turns out she's seen me before.

"I wondered how you stayed so thin! I saw you at BonJour and thought you probably got away with eating like a pig."

Things are picking up—someone on my wavelength who looks like she has a brain and sense of humor.

Roberta introduces some changes in my plan of action. She has no use for Sustagen, and shows me how she pours it into her oblong knitting container and then down the toilet. She has absolutely no intention of putting on an extra pound, and initiates our meals of iceberg lettuce doused with ketchup. We share a stash of chewing gum and predilections, such as trying to dress well in spite of all the odds. Roberta's a designer; the way things look is key.

She thinks I'm just like her, a non-eater. I wonder how she'll react when I tell her what I do. If I tell her.

A tragic moment: Roberta put on weight without having eaten anything! How can it be? Could it be gas? She'll ask her doctor husband but doubts he'll have the answer. She can't ask a shrink.

I tell her about Frank. She's jealous. She's not crazy about her doctor husband.

"Never marry a doctor of any description. You're lucky he's a lawyer. I love lawyers who sue doctors, especially if they're shrinks. Maybe we can build up a case; there's sure to be a reason."

See what I mean about a sense of humor? Except she's probably not joking.

Taia, Lucy, Linda, Bonnie—what are they doing here? I don't have a clue. What could they have done or not done? Especially Bonnie, with her cute smile. I'll try to get to know her better. Roberta's the only one here I can understand.

Frank will be here soon, and that's the only thing that counts.

❊ ❊ ❊

A FLURRY OF ACTIVITY on the ward. A couple of doctors come rushing in, and an attendant wheels in a huge oxygen cylinder.

Turns out Mrs. Goldblatt tried to kill herself. Maybe she ran out of plastic.

Cut that out. It's not funny.

She's out of danger. The doctors look exasperated.

What a pain in the neck, pulling a suicide stunt while they're on their lunch break.

Later Mrs. Goldblatt tells me she got a good scolding. She didn't tell me what she did, and I didn't ask.

Put a plastic bag over her head? Cut that out.

The ward is back to normal, if you'll pardon the expression. The pacers are pacing, the mutes are mute, Nina is glued to a cartoon on the TV, Linda and Bonnie are playing checkers, Taia and Lucy are off in a corner (are they in love?) and Roberta and I are chewing gum and discussing her love life. It stinks.

Dinner time. It's some sort of noodle and fish casserole, very messy and loaded with calories. I'm not even hungry. Roberta and I create our lettuce and ketchup salad combinations, all is well until: Fatso waddles in, preceded by her distinct aroma. Somehow they've kept her out of our way before.

Roberta goes off like a time bomb.

"If you can't get that fat mess out of here I promise I'll be sick all over the dining room table."

Fatso is unmoved. Likely she's heard something like this before.

Even louder, which I didn't think possible:

"It's bad enough it's in the area, but allowing it into this room while we're attempting to eat a meal is—I want the doctor on call!"

"Get the damn doctor on call or get that fat disgrace out of here! This minute!"

They escort Fatso out. Everyone applauds. Roberta bows, and we eat our salads.

❊ ❊ ❊

It's SATURDAY, AND FRANK arrives, looking as happy as usual. We sit on the corridor bench as he tells me news of the outside world…his work with Ed Logue at the Redevelopment Agency, the changing Boston waterfront and new Faneuil Hall Marketplace…Martin Luther King and the civil rights movement…what's he doing here, with me?

He'll spend the night at 90th Street and see me in the morning.

At night the sound of children crying. Is their ward one floor up or down?

HE'S GONE, AND HAS Reserve duty next weekend. I'll have to wait two weeks.

I should get a calendar. What difference do the days make?

I'm hungry.

Here I go again. How to get food?

The high points of our days: morning rounds, OT and, of course, volley ball. Doctor Mendelson, the head psychiatrist, leads the morning rounds. He has a commanding presence and straightforward manner. These guys are not into Freudian pussyfooting, thank goodness.

Will that make a difference? Of course it will. Think of Frank and think positive.

Mendelson does not appreciate sarcasm, so I control my wit. Except for an occasional lapse.

"How are you this morning?" he asks.

"Very good," I smile politely. "And how are you today?"

"Miss Seidner," he glares, "I understand that" followed up with some psychiatric put-down, such as "you're skipping meals but organizing pastry runs."

How does he know? It's true. Bingeing is tricky but not impossible. My pal Linda has been indispensable; she has off-ward privileges and was easily persuaded. She seems to enjoy the smuggling process, and actually managed to bring in a whole cake hidden under her raincoat, smiling triumphantly.

I'm not as amused as she is. I'm scared.

Hey Mendelson, I may not show it but I'm really scared. Can you help me?

NOVEMBER 22, 1963 —

President Kennedy has been shot! Everything stops. President Kennedy is dead. A few nurses cry. The rest of us, mute, watch the funeral on TV. The world penetrates those thick gray walls for a few days, but then it disappears.

❊ ❊ ❊

[From Psychiatric Institute Medical Records]
Marian Seidner; Six Weeks Summary (December, 1963)

At college Marian developed an air of indifference and superficiality which apparently made her a hit at cocktail parties but a failure at sustained relationships...

...We know little of the genetic features here, however, the patient's parents have insisted that the patient's illness is genetic in origin. There is a history of a series of suicides on the maternal side of the family; the details concerning these events are being clarified...

Therapeutic Formulation

Goals in treatment are to help the patient establish her identity just as soon as feasible...A period of in-patient treatment with firm controls would seem to be important...

❊ ❊ ❊

I LIKE DOCTOR WHARTON. The best thing about our sessions is what he doesn't do: he doesn't stare at me as if I'm one of Freud's hysterics ready to reenact the dreadful secret of my past. He doesn't expect me to hate my father and regret my mother, and he doesn't dismiss my humor as a big cover-up.

What if it is?

Mrs. Goldblatt, Fatso, Nina glued to the TV—I'd rather laugh than cry, if you don't mind.

The sound of children crying in the night –there's nothing funny about that. But let's not even think about it.

Okay, okay, I'm making headway. If someone says "Marian" I'm not surprised I have a name. Thanks, Doctor Wharton.

But I'm still hungrier than ever and I'm scared.

Another Christmas comes and goes and it's 1964. No one here makes New Year's Resolutions.

❋ ❋ ❋

At last: privileges to leave the hospital with Frank!

Euphoria. He arrives Friday evening, we drive to 90th Street, and we hit the town. The Rainbow Room, Elaine's, or just swinging down Park Avenue—it really doesn't matter—we're together and we're free. Our weekends make the week worthwhile.

Now that they've moved Roberta down to an open ward it's kind of lonely. Taia and Lucy are always together, it's hard to get Nina away from the TV, Linda and Bonnie are really nice—I like them both—but they're on a different wavelength. Linda's been great helping me out with food, and even Nina has pitched in, getting candy from the downstairs machine. Bonnie tends to stay by herself, but she opened up a little, when I sat next to her in OT.

"Bonnie, that's really nice—how'd you get it so symmetrical?" She was working so intently, and the pot was quite impressive.

"Thanks, Marian, I find it helps to try and sit still and concentrate."

"Helps?—I mean, you're probably the least crazy-seeming person on the floor—in fact, what the hell are you doing here anyway?"

A big smile. "Marian, that just goes to show. You should have seen me without the medication—a regular basket case." Smoothing the clay, "I've wondered about you, but I guess you're just an eating problem, right?"

Bonnie likes to look over my shoulder when I draw.

"Marian, that's so good. Could you do a card for my little sister's birthday?" She's so happy with my dopey card it makes me want to cry.

Group Therapy: Everybody's sitting around in a circle, and somehow, I don't know why, I find myself talking about my secret eating and vomiting binges…I can't believe I'm doing it. And I can't believe the reaction: *zero*. Nobody bats an eye; it's no big deal. It's nowhere near as dramatic as everyone else's problems.

Maybe I'm not as hopeless as I think I am.

Bonnie's anxiety attacks, Nina's drug use, Taia's gender identification—that's worth some serious discussion. Marian, get over it, you think you have problems? Listen to ours.

Things are looking up.

❋ ❋ ❋

DOCTOR BRUCH HAS BEEN a background consultant on my case. She surfaces: "Marian, would you be willing to appear before one of my classes to answer some questions?"

"Of course!"

This is a far cry from my starring role as Cassie, but as close to the stage as I can get at P.I.

When my big day as a case study arrives, I'm led into a large room filled with medical students. They stare at me and I smile back, in my least crazy way.

Doctor Bruch starts.

"Marian, could you tell us the two most important causes of your illness?"

Easy question.

"Being a twin, and the war."

Being a twin: lots of attention, never lonely, but not easy. We knew our differences, but no one else did. We were dressed alike, grew up expecting stares and adulation, and accepted being so hard to tell apart that I had to show the mole on my hand to prove who I was. My parents knew: I was the moody one with a nasty temper, whereas Susan was the good one with a sunny disposition. Whether it was nature or nurture, we played our assigned roles to the hilt.

The war: It affected my life because of the impact it had on my parents. As a young child, I sensed my parents were afraid; there was no feeling of security. Although my parents spoke English fluently and we lived comfortably, they never really adjusted, always acutely aware of what they had lost. I grew up feeling sorry for them, and wishing they would disappear.

Everyone seemed pleased by my response, which elicited more questions and answers. Obviously satisfied by my performance, Doctor Bruch thanked me and led me out.

Whoops, I totally forgot another likely factor: genetics. Medical history on my mother's side? Can't say, because they all killed themselves: My maternal grandmother, her sister, and my mother's two brothers. In my experience, more attention was paid to the Rorschach than to the family tree. Probably a good thing McLean overlooked it.

❄ ❄ ❄

Life on the ward continues at pretty much the same pace, but the days are getting warmer. Weekends with Frank are more relaxed; the city in summer slows down.

Summer? Already?

If I'm making such "good progress" how come I'm still at it? What can I do to get control? Does anybody know how scared I really am, aside from me?

After Frank leaves, it's hard to sleep. I hear footsteps, children crying, distant whispering.

No point in lying there. I get up, find my slippers, head for the corridor with *Time Magazine*—the bench near the nurses' station is pretty well lit.

Bonnie's in trouble. She's shaking, pacing the hall, shaking, shaking like I've never seen before. I go to her, try to talk, hope I can calm her.

"They've taken away my meds. I need my medication." Pointing to the nurses' station. "She won't listen." She tries again. The answer: "Sorry, no. Doctor's orders."

I stay a while and try to talk with her, but there's nothing I can do. I go to bed.

A few days later Bonnie manages to get away and kills herself by jumping off the George Washington Bridge.

"And I am shaken; but not as a leaf."

The minute the news hits the ward Mendelson schedules a meeting of all patients and staff. Suicides can be contagious.

"I will be brief,
Assuredly I have a grief,
And I am shaken; but not as a leaf."

He gives a long speech, reassuring us that all will be well: we are getting excellent care, unfortunate incidents notwithstanding. There is weeping in the room.

"Sorry, no. Doctor's orders."

We are asked to express our concerns.

"I need my medication."

"Sorry, no. Doctor's orders."

I ask questions.

"Why didn't Bonnie get the help she needed when her meds were cut off? Since she was clearly having panic attacks why wasn't anyone attending to her?"

Doctor Mendelson responds.

"You wouldn't know, listening to Miss Seidner, that all she really thinks about is food."

I look around the room. They don't look back.

They're all staring straight ahead.

The bastard.

"Don't let the bastards get you down—don't let the bastards get you down—don't let..."

What about Bonnie?

The next day I'm told I'm "too upset" to leave for the weekend. Frank is on his way down, and I'm restricted to the ward.

That does it. I escape from the Occupational Therapy Room.

Bonnie's pot is gone.

Miss Cronin trusts me, and doesn't even turn her head as I walk out. Out, as far as she's concerned, to go to the bathroom at the end of the hall. I walk to the elevator, get in, push ten, get out on the ground floor, to the main entrance and into the street.

Uh-oh. I have a problem: a ward nurse has noticed and is right behind me.

I start to run, and so does she.

This is really happening: I'm running up Fort Washington Avenue with a nurse in a white uniform chasing me at a good clip.

This is insane.

I stop running and sit on the curb, where she joins me for a cigarette. We return to the ward together.

TIME'S UP

More days, more group therapy, more volleyball, more bingeing, more weekends with Frank.

It's Labor Day weekend; we have an extra day together! We're in our favorite little restaurant, Puchetta's, just down the street on 88th and Third. He's eating and I'm drinking.

"Marian, you realize—it's been a year."

I know and I'm scared. He's never scared of anything…maybe he's right, but how would I know?

Frank, don't you understand? I keep telling you: I haven't really changed!

"I'm still as bad as ever."

"Well, they've had a year to change you. Now we're getting married. Time to leave the P.I."

I'm scared to go, but terrified of staying.

Poor Bonnie. I'm just scared…imagine how she felt. Don't even think about it.

"I'm scared."

He just smiles and keeps on eating.

❈ ❈ ❈

DOCTOR MENDELSON CALLS A conference. Frank and my parents join me in a meeting room, where we're surrounded by social workers, a couple of nurses, and Mendelson, who starts things off. He describes the progress I've made: more self-awareness, openness and compliance with the staff…

Blah, blah, sure, sure, so what?

But, he continues, there's still work to be done before I'm ready for discharge.

What the hell kind of work? The work isn't working.

At the worst, he says, I'll stick my head in an oven and blow up everyone I live with.

What!?

I try to say something but he tells me to be quiet. It's Frank's turn.

Frank says Mendelson's approach is that of a doctor, but he's a lawyer. In the allotted year not enough has changed to warrant my staying any longer. Furthermore, as far as the gas oven is concerned, he'll take his chances. We've given the hospital one year, the year is up, and we're leaving.

I'm a voluntary patient; they have no choice but to discharge me when I sign myself out. Mendelson insists to the end I'm not ready to leave alone. He has a nurse escort me to my freedom.

❀ ❀ ❀

[From Psychiatric Institute Medical Records]

Marian Seidner

Admitted: 10/2/63

Discharged: 9/15/64

Discharge Summary

Marian Seidner is a 29 year-old, single, white identical twin who was admitted to the Psychiatric Institute for the first time on October 2, 1963, with chief complaints of compulsive overeating followed by self-induced vomiting associated with weight loss and marked weakness, and depression and suicidal ideation, all of eight to nine year's duration.

On physical examination patient appeared to be an attractive, essentially normal young woman except for marked underweight and associated weakness. Laboratory data was essentially normal except for a subtle thinking disorder and mild depression.

Initial treatment included complete restrictions on the ward and supplementation of nutrition with Sustagen and vitamins. The initial goal in psychotherapy was to aid patient in establishing an identity of herself separate from her twin. On the ward she was always openly compliant and pleasant, and had difficulty expressing any hostile feelings. With controls her overeating stopped. As soon as controls were slackened she became anxious, her overeating would return, and she would cease functioning. Her anxiety was also increased by her approaching marriage and her fears of incompetence, which she projected on the hospital. She was able to reorganize to some extent her pattern of feeling inadequate, becoming anxious, then overeating and having her anxiety diminish. However, she became increasingly unwilling to remain in the hospital for treatment. Because her fiancé was unconcerned by her overeating, and because he provided the structure, control and security she needed, it was felt that marriage to him might help her live within manageable limits with her symptoms.

The diagnosis was anorexia nervosa...The patient was discharged as improved.

Discharged: September 15, 1964, to self.

Diagnosis: PSYCHONEUROSIS, ANOREXIA NERVOSA

Condition: IMPROVED

Approved By: Allen Mendelson, M.D./Hbc

Postscripts

We got married in New York City Hall in October 1964, along with a diverse group of couples, with and without children. My sister Susan and Frank's brother Joe were our witnesses. I tried hard not to laugh when the city official pronounced us married "in the name of the City of New York," but it was a great day and a major turning point.

The bingeing continued, but so did our lives. We adopted two children as newborns, Richard and Angela, two years apart. My love for my children transcended everything. The binges began to decrease, and finally disappeared.

Lily Michaels stayed in McLean the longest. Her parents finally had her transferred to another hospital, where she was discharged after shock therapy. Lily's mother landed up at McLean with a clinical depression. Her younger sister committed suicide. My attempts to stay in touch failed; Lily was clearly trying to break all ties with her past.

Laura Weaver successfully settled her lawsuit with McLean, divorced, re-married, and moved to West Virginia, where she is living happily ever after. We stay in touch.

Barbara Raye was always a mystery; she still is.

Dan Hughes committed suicide in 1964.

Ellen Rangler and I re-connected more than ten years later, when we both sent our children to the Belmont Day School. Our McLean days seemed part of the distant past; we were now concerned with kids and car pools. Ellen killed herself by turning the car engine on in her closed garage.

Roberta Parnas divorced her husband, got a nose job, and, according to my sister, who bumped into her in New York, was working as a textile designer and looked terrific.

I continued to correspond with Doctor Bruch, who left New York for Baylor College of Medicine in Houston, Texas. I appear in her book, *Eating Disorders*, under a fictitious name. Hilde Bruch died in 1984.

Questions and Answers

Why me?

I still don't know. There was plenty of love and respect in my family. I had a great education, many friends, and all the opportunities I could dream of.

Do I really believe my problems were the result of being a twin or the war?

No.

Could they be the result of a chemical or genetic quirk?

Research will tell, but not in my lifetime.

Your treatment at McLean?

We were being pampered in a never-never-land of Freudian hogwash. Those of us who made a successful exit did so, by and large, by recognizing the futility of staying.

Although talk therapy undoubtedly is helpful to the troubled, it has, in my experience, never by itself cured a member of the mentally ill.

Too much money changed hands.

And Psychiatric Institute?

I was lucky; I got out by marrying a great guy who didn't know enough to be scared off by my problems or their prognosis. I was able to get out, get a life, and recover.

Bonnie jumped off the George Washington Bridge.

Any advice for others?

No.

Made in the USA
Columbia, SC
19 April 2021